FINDING THEIR VOICES:
LISTENING TO BATTERED WOMEN WHO'VE KILLED

FINDING THEIR VOICES:
LISTENING TO BATTERED WOMEN WHO'VE KILLED

AMY L. BUSCH

Kroshka Books
Commack, New York

Editorial Production:	Susan Boriotti
Office Manager:	Annette Hellinger
Graphics:	Frank Grucci and John T'Lustachowski
Information Editor:	Tatiana Shohov
Book Production:	Donna Dennis, Patrick Davin, Christine Mathosian and Tammy Sauter
Circulation:	Maryanne Schmidt
Marketing/Sales:	Cathy DeGregory

Library of Congress Cataloging-in-Publication Data
Busch, Amy Lou.
    Finding their voices: listening to battered women who've killed / Amy Lou Busch.
      p.   cm.
    Includes bibliographical references and index.
    ISBN 1-56072-618-0
    1. Abused women--Crimes against--United States. 2. Abused women--Legal status, laws. etc.--United States. 3. Wife abuse-- United States. 4. Battered woman syndrome--United States. 5. Abusive men--United States--Mortality. 6. Justifiable homicide--United States. I. Title.
HV6626.2.B37   1998   98-43163
364.15'23'0820973--dc21   CIP

Copyright © 1999 by Amy Lou Busch
    Kroshka Books, a division of
    Nova Science Publishers, Inc.
    6080 Jericho Turnpike, Suite 207
    Commack, New York 11725
    Tele. 516-499-3103   Fax 516-499-3146
    e-mail: Novascience@earthlink.net
    e-mail: Novascil@aol.com
    Web Site: http://www.nexusworld.com/nova

All rights reserved. No part of this book may be reproduced, stored in a retrieval system or transmitted in any form or by any means: electronic, electrostatic, magnetic, tape, mechanical photocopying, recording or otherwise without permission from the publishers.
The authors and publisher have taken care in preparation of this book, but make no expressed or implied warranty of any kind and assume no responsibility for any errors or omissions. No liability is assumed for incidental or consequential damages in connection with or arising out of information contained in this book.
This publication is designed to provide accurate and authoritative information with regard to the subject matter covered herein. It is sold with the clear understanding that the publisher is not engaged in rendering legal or any other professional services. If legal or any other expert assistance is required, the services of a competent person should be sought. FROM A DECLARATION OF PARTICIPANTS JOINTLY ADOPTED BY A COMMITTEE OF THE AMERICAN BAR ASSOCIATION AND A COMMITTEE OF PUBLISHERS.

Printed in the United States of America

Contents

ACKNOWLEDGMENTS _____ VII

PREFACE _____ IX

INTRODUCTION _____ XI
    LISA _____ XI
    SHANNON _____ XII
    PATRICIA _____ XIII
    ELAINE _____ XIV

BACKGROUND AND METHODOLOGY _____ 1
    THE RESEARCHER _____ 2
    THE STUDY _____ 2
    THE THEORY _____ 4
    THE METHODOLOGY _____ 6

SELF-DEFENSE AND CLEMENCY: CLASSIFYING
BATTERED WOMEN WHO KILL _____ 11
    BATTERED WOMEN AND THE LAW _____ 12
    WHEN A WOMAN KILLS _____ 14
    SELF-DEFENSE _____ 16
    CLEMENCY _____ 23
    MERCY OR EQUITY? _____ 25

THE BATTERED WOMAN SYNDROME: CHALLENGES
TO THE THEORY _____ 29
    THE BATTERED WOMAN _____ 30
    THE BATTERED WOMAN SYNDROME _____ 34
    THE CYCLE OF VIOLENCE _____ 34
    LEARNED HELPLESSNESS _____ 37
    A FLAWED THEORY _____ 38

ALTERNATIVES TO LEARNED HELPLESSNESS___42

SELF-REPRESENTATIONS OF BATTERED WOMEN WHO KILLED___47
　　REDEFINITION___48
　　VALIDATION OF VICTIMIZATION___50
　　VICTIMS, AGAIN?___51
　　FROM VICTIMS TO SURVIVORS___53
　　THE BATTERED WOMAN SYNDROME___54
　　LEARNED HELPLESSNESS___55
　　WHY DIDN'T THEY LEAVE?___57
　　JUSTICE___63

CONCLUSION___69

EPILOGUE___73

THE BATTERED WOMAN SYNDROME: FIVE YEARS LATER___73
　　POSTTRAUMATIC STRESS DISORDER___74
　　RATES OF DOMESTIC VIOLENCE – THE CURRENT PICTURE___78
　　THE FEDERAL RESPONSE TO PARTNER VIOLENCE___79
　　BATTERED WOMEN'S SELF-DEFENSE – FIVE YEARS LATER___80
　　THE WOMEN'S STORIES: FIVE YEARS LATER___81
　　JUSTICE: FIVE YEARS LATER___82

ABOUT THE AUTHOR___83

BIBLIOGRAPHY___83
　　BOOKS___83
　　ARTICLES___84
　　GOVERNMENT PUBLICATIONS___88
　　LEGAL DOCUMENTS___89
　　CASES___89
　　OTHER SOURCES___90

ACKNOWLEDGMENTS

I owe thanks to Suzanne Kirschner, who guided my project at Harvard and encouraged me to pursue my interest in clinical psychology. Lisa Goodman inspired me to dust off my manuscript and demonstrated, by example, the potential contribution of thoughtful domestic violence research. Thanks also to Juliet Eilperin, who painstakingly reviewed my manuscript; to Andrew Criss, who contributed his unsurpassed creativity; and to Kevin, who greatly improved this work and inspired me to keep going. Most of all, I am grateful to the four women who entrusted me with their stories.

PREFACE

This book is based on a project I began in 1993 as an undergraduate at Harvard University. While I have updated the text to reflect the theoretical and practical advances that have since been made in the area of domestic violence, I have also taken care to preserve the women's stories within the context they were originally told.

INTRODUCTION

LISA

And being beaten, you also, at a certain point in time, when you're being beaten, you have flashbacks of other bad times, and one was worse than the other, so you start thinking of what could happen. And I used to tell Tommy just to kill me, because I just wanted it over with. I just wanted it to end. So when those two guys offered. . . .

Well, you know, it built up with — they started coming in to where I worked, and they saw me being abused by Tommy, and they saw him threatening me at work, giving me a hard time, punching me in the mouth, cutting my leather up, telling me it was gonna be my face. So they watched this stuff, and these are macho guys, and so they said, "You know, Lisa, this is crazy, let us just tell him, you know, we'll break his legs, we'll beat him up." And I listened to this for a month's time, and Tommy was constantly at my door, trying to break in, and I had another restraining order on him, of which I had many, and so when these guys offered one night, and it had been so bad with Tommy those past few days, with what he did to me, that I said O.K. You know, I wanted Tommy to feel what I felt. And that doesn't justify what happened to him, but I just wanted him to feel what happened to me.

I was angry, and I was terrified of him. I was terrified of him. I mean, I would keep my doors locked, my windows locked and nailed shut, in the midst of summer, you know, I was deathly afraid of this man. So these two guys offered again, and I took them up. I went and got him from work, and I made him think that I was going to have sex with him, and I wasn't. But in my mind, I didn't think that the end result was going to be death, either. I wanted him to be beaten up. But the end result was death.

Well, the guys, when they got back in the car, they said that they beat him up with bats, and one guy turned to the other and said, "I kept hitting him," and I wasn't thinking that he was dead, I wasn't thinking anything. I felt numb. I was sick to my stomach, I threw up, I don't know. And then, when I was arrested for murder, it was almost a relief to me.[1]

Lisa Grimshaw is a 28-year-old white woman, and the mother of two children.[2] In 1986, she was tried for murder and convicted of manslaughter and conspiracy to commit murder. Lisa's two male friends had killed her husband with baseball bats; one pleaded guilty to the charges in return for a 15-year sentence, but the other did not receive any jail time at all. Lisa was given a 15- to 20-year sentence.

SHANNON

All the time I was with José he had a gun and was dealing drugs. He threatened me with a gun on Easter Sunday in 1989, the week before he died. He put a gun to my head and threatened to kill me. He said, "Bitch, I'll kill you before you leave me." I called my aunt and told her about this. I told her if something happens to me, José did it. Later he said he loved me and started to cry.

A week later, José and Shannon were arguing, and he began to beat her:

He had his gun, he put the gun in the drawer. I thought, "He's really gonna kill me now." He was still cussing. I was crying. He jumped on me and was choking me on the bed. Telling me I'm no good. I asked, "Why do you put me through these changes, you know I love you?" He was smacking me. He told me to get out of his life. I said, "O.K." and started to put my things together. He said, "No, you're not going." And he said he would kill me before he left. When he was out of the room, I had put the gun under the mattress. When he came back he looked for

---

[1] Lisa Grimshaw, interview by author, tape recording, Lancaster, MA, 17 June 1993.
[2] The women's ages are as of the time of interview.

the gun. He asked me where it was. I did not tell him. He told me to leave but we started fighting again. He hit me in the face and started choking me. I pulled the gun out, I shot him in the head. I asked him if he was all right. He said, "You shot me in the head bitch, I'm going to kill you." I don't remember the other shots, just the first one.[3]

Shannon Booker is a 26-year-old African-American woman, and the mother of two children. Charged with second-degree murder for shooting her boyfriend José with his own gun, on February 21, 1990, Shannon pleaded guilty to manslaughter and received an 8- to 15-year prison sentence.

PATRICIA

After her divorce from Brian Hennessy, Patricia says the harassment continued. Patricia had received custody of her son, Timmy, but one day a substitute judge, unfamiliar with the case, granted a month of custody to Timmy's father in Florida:

I was having a nervous breakdown. I told my lawyer to do something, anything. Timmy was not going to Florida, no way. I'll never see him again. He'll die. I'll die. If I tell Brian "No" (God forbid), he'll kill me, he'll take Timmy, he'll kill us both. What am I going to do? What? Where could I go? I had nowhere to go. I didn't want to go. I had lost everything I worked all my life for the last time I had to run from him. I was just getting my life in order again. There's no end to this. It will never be over. I should just kill myself. I was in a panic. I was confused, upset, mad, memories of all *his* abuse.

I go to the cabinet. I reach in, feel a gun. I take it and go to the porch door. I open it. I walk out. My heart's beating out of my chest. I raise the gun. Brian sees it. There goes his smug little smile . . . Brian knew he pushed me too far. It was him or me. I couldn't breathe. There was no air. It was like heavy syrup. He has to stop. I have to stop him. I don't want to die. Turn the gun in on yourself and shoot. No, yes, no. It's time.

---

[3] Shannon Booker, Personal Statement to the Governor and Parole Board: Clemency Petition, 14 February 1992, 7-9.

I pulled the trigger.[4]

Patricia Hennessy is 31 years old, white, and the mother of an 11-year-old son. In 1988, she shot her ex-husband with a gun belonging to her father, a retired police officer. Charged with first-degree murder, she pleaded guilty to manslaughter. She received a near-maximum sentence of 18 to 20 years in prison.

ELAINE

The second time I called the police I asked them if they would charge Jerry with assault and battery. They said they couldn't because they hadn't witnessed him abuse me. They wouldn't make my husband leave, and he hurt me so bad afterwards that I couldn't leave the house for two days. I'll never forget that beating because he had been throwing beer bottles at me, and the broken glass cut my feet up pretty bad when I was running away from him. He finally caught me and punched me in the nose and repeatedly punched me in the stomach, legs and back. After knocking me down, he dragged me by the hair across the room over the broken glass to the kitchen. When we got to the kitchen he ordered me to cook him something to eat "or else." I had glass in my feet and body for days. After that, I didn't bother calling the police again.

Then that dreadful day came. It was different than any other night of abuse that I had experienced. My husband had come home heavily intoxicated and acted like he was high on cocaine. He scared me that night, chasing me around the apartment and yelling that it was all my fault he was in trouble. Jerry started striking me and I fled from one room to another to escape him. I tried to get out the window at one point, but he caught me and flung me across the room with a back-hand. I got to my feet and headed towards the front door and he blocked it. I got away and tried to get out the window and he started to strangle me and somehow I got away again. The next time he caught me I knew he was going to kill me. Somehow he had

---

[4] Patricia Hennessy, Personal Statement to the Governor and Parole Board: Clemency Petition, 14 February 1992, 10.

me trapped in the hallway which adjoined the dining room. Striking me, and bouncing my body against the wall, we struggled. He said he was going to kill me and had a cold look in his eyes and started beating my body and my head against the wall. My heart started beating so fast I could feel it in my throat. He was picking me up over his head to throw me against the wall. All I could visualize was hitting the wall and never getting up again.

While he was doing all this he repeatedly said he was going to kill me. As I was going off the ground all I could think of was stopping him. At that moment I reached out to grab something off the dining room table while my feet were off the ground and found something and struck him. I don't know what I hit him with because a split second later I hit the wall. Or should I say my whole body and head hit the wall with such impact that it knocked me out.[5]

On April 26th, 1985, Elaine Hyde was arrested for the stabbing death of her husband. During their five years of marriage, Elaine was verbally abused, beaten, kicked, raped, locked in closets, and threatened with death. However, these stories of violence were not admitted at her trial. Convicted of manslaughter, Elaine was sentenced to 10 to 20 years in prison. On February 14, 1992, she and seven other Massachusetts women requested clemency from Governor Weld, contending that they were suffering from the battered woman syndrome when they killed their abusers.

Violence against women is not a new phenomenon in American society, but it has only recently received public attention. In the 1960s, the women's movement brought many changes in the areas of law and social policy; prominent among them was the psychological and legal community's articulation and examination of issues surrounding domestic violence. In the years that have followed, the term "battered woman" has become an accepted descriptive label for a woman who experiences abuse within an intimate relationship.

Although scholars have proposed various theories to describe the perceptions and behavior of battered women, one has remained the most influential. Lenore Walker, a leading psychologist in the field of domestic

---

[5] Elaine Hyde, Personal Statement to the Governor and Parole Board: Clemency Petition, 13-4.

violence, wrote *The Battered Woman* in 1979.[6] Her theory, the battered woman syndrome, responded to the question most frequently asked about these women: "Why don't they just leave?" Drawing from interviews and stories of over 400 battered women, Lenore Walker developed a psychosocial theory of the effects of prolonged abuse on a woman and how they act together to prevent her from escaping a battering relationship. The battered woman syndrome was intended to dispel a common misconception, fueled by Freudian notions of female masochism, that women enjoy the abuse or exaggerate its severity; it describes battered women as victims who are incapable of escape.[7]

Recently, wife abuse has become a "hot topic;" talk shows and journalists are now focusing on battered women and their sensational stories of violence. The trial of O. J. Simpson brought the issue into the living rooms of America. As a result, a certain group of battered women, those who have killed their abusers, are rapidly gaining recognition. Changes in the law, highlighted by battered women's self-defense and clemency cases, reflect an assumption by judges, legislators, and members of the general public that the "crimes" committed by these women should be viewed differently than other offenses. Recent legal defense of battered women who have killed has centered on the battered woman syndrome.[8]

Although the battered woman syndrome has been hailed as a valuable legal instrument for women who have killed their abusers, some scholars contend that the theory is flawed. Several essential questions have filtered out of this debate. Is the battered woman syndrome a suitable theoretical category in which to place these women, their experiences, and their acts of killing? How do the women feel about the labels that have been placed on their lives and behavior by others? Do they feel that they should be excused based on their past victimization? And finally, what would constitute justice in the cases of battered women who kill? This work attempts to address these questions.

---

[6] Lenore Walker, *The Battered Woman* (New York: Harper & Row, 1979). Lenore Walker subsequently published several other books and many articles on domestic violence. See e.g., Lenore Walker, *The Battered Woman Syndrome* (New York: Springer Publishing, 1984), and Lenore Walker, *Terrifying Love* (New York: Harper & Row, 1989).

[7] For further discussion of the use of the battered woman syndrome to dispel common misconceptions about abused women, see Edward Gondolf and Ellen Fisher, *Battered Women as Survivors: An Alternative to Treating Learned Helplessness* (Lexington, MA: D.C. Heath, 1988), 14-5, 19; and Diane Follingstad et al., "Factors Predicting Verdicts Where Battered Women Kill Their Husbands," *Law and Human Behavior* 13.3 (1989): 256.

[8] Since 1977, Lenore Walker alone has testified on the battered woman syndrome in more than 150 murder trials throughout the United States. See Walker, *Terrifying Love*, 7

In Chapter One, I discuss the value commitments and methodological premises that have guided my project and its conclusions. In Chapter Two, I describe the principles of self-defense law and how they have traditionally discriminated against battered women who kill their abusers. I then introduce the battered woman syndrome as a theory intended to describe the perceptions and behavior of these women as reasonable before the law. Having gradually gained acceptance with most state courts, the battered woman syndrome also has become an instrument for reviewing the cases of women already convicted of killing their abusers. In the second part of the chapter, I attempt to shed light on some of the issues and problems associated with clemency for incarcerated battered women. Specifically, I explore the distinction between a commutation and a pardon and its relationship to justice in the cases of battered women who have killed.

In Chapter Three, I examine the battered woman syndrome in greater detail, focusing on the theoretical debate surrounding its accuracy and legal utility for battered women who have defended their lives. Some legal scholars warn against the potential misconstruction of a "syndrome" to describe these women within the courts. They suggest that unless defense attorneys present it cautiously, the theory may actually preclude some women from being judged as reasonable actors within the law of self-defense. I argue, however, that the battered woman syndrome requires more than careful articulation. The theory must be reformulated to present a more accurate and legally valuable description of battered women's behavior. In the final section of that chapter, I present two social theories as alternatives to the psychological construct of the battered woman syndrome. One emphasizes the forces within society that may prevent a woman from leaving an abusive relationship, while the other highlights the risk of retaliation a woman faces when attempting to separate from a violent partner.

The few studies that exist on battered women who have killed focus on what psychologists, attorneys, and academics have to say about their conduct. To date, there has been no study of how the women perceive themselves and their actions, and how they feel about the labels that have been applied to them. I believe that the voices of women who have killed their abusers must be brought into this debate. My work is founded on the conviction that the life stories of these women can inform the theory used to describe them, illuminating disjunctions between the battered woman syndrome and their own explanations for their actions. By revealing the social and legal constraints that have shaped the women's behavior, these stories indicate factors that society and the criminal justice system should consider when pronouncing judgment on battered women and their "crimes." In the final chapter of this book, I explore the ways in which the battered woman syndrome has influenced the women's conceptions of their experiences and actions, and I examine the relevance of each element of this theory to their life stories. I conclude the chapter with an investigation into the meaning of justice for battered women who have killed.

My work suggests that some aspects of the battered woman syndrome conflict with battered women's actual experiences and fail to adequately account for their acts of killing. In examining the stories of four of these women, a theory emerges that contradicts the passive, helpless implications of the syndrome theory and portrays these women, correctly, as survivors of life-threatening circumstances. Viewed in this light, these women's "crimes" may be considered within the realm of justified self-defense.

CHAPTER ONE

BACKGROUND AND METHODOLOGY

> Feminist scholars have studied women, men, and social relations between the genders within, across, and insistently against the frameworks of the disciplines. In each area we have come to understand that what we took to be humanly inclusive problematics, concepts, theories, objective methodologies, and transcendental truths are in fact far less than that. Instead, these products of thought bear the mark of their collective and individual creators, and the creators in turn have been distinctively marked as to gender, class, race, and culture.
>
> –Sandra Harding,
> *The Science Question in Feminism*[9]

Deftly and effectively, recent feminist scholarship has challenged mainstream social science's claim to objectivity: the assumption that research can be conducted from a neutral perspective, and that the resulting findings are the unbiased "truth." According to this perspective, the values of the researcher inform every element of a study, from the research goals to the methodology used. In traditional social science, while claiming neutrality, these values have tended to support a patriarchal, androcentric view of society and family relations. For this reason, feminist social theorists encourage examination of the relationship

---

[9] Sandra Harding, *The Science Question in Feminism* (Ithaca: Cornell University Press, 1986), 15.

between the researcher, the topic chosen for study, the theory that directs the research, and the methodology that is employed.

Feminist scholars argue that it is crucial to set forth the values that determine the issues to be explored and to position the researcher as an interacting element in the project. Feminists do not claim to be value-free; values are inherent in all research. Values perpetually exist and influence; what is most harmful to a project is a failure to acknowledge this fact. Agreeing with these principles, I feel that it is essential to uncover the assumptions that have guided my work with battered women who killed their abusers. The topic, questions, theory, and methodology that have directed my project all necessarily derive from my own perspective on violence against women in our society.

THE RESEARCHER

I first became interested in the issue of domestic violence during the Spring of 1992, when I worked with battered women in New York City. My job at a social service agency was to locate attorneys willing to represent battered women seeking orders of protection, divorce, and custody proceedings against their abusive partners. Needless to say, the work was demoralizing, both because so few lawyers were willing to perform this service on a pro bono basis, and because for so many of these women, a legal document offered little real protection. The women told me numerous stories of police who had failed to get involved in their "domestic disputes," housing authorities who answered their requests for alternative shelter with nine-month waiting lists, and a court system that functioned more like an obstacle course than an effective judicial remedy for their situations. Listening to these women, I was struck by their repeatedly frustrated efforts to leave their abusive partners for safety. I began to view battered women not as isolated individuals suffering from psychological defects, but as women working against tremendous legal, economic, and social constraints. I no longer asked why these women remained with their batterers; instead, I sought to understand why society tolerated domestic crimes and gave so many battered women no other alternative but to fight back.

THE STUDY

In March of 1993, I learned of the Framingham Eight: eight women in Massachusetts' Framingham Correctional Institution who had been convicted of killing their abusers in the late 1980s.[10] These women were appealing to the Governor of Massachusetts for clemency. After contacting their attorneys and officials at the prison, I was given permission to meet and interview four of these women.[11] Three of the women are white and one is African-American. When we met, they ranged in age from 26 to 40. They come from various socio-economic classes. Elaine graduated from high school, but none of the women have college degrees. Elaine and Lisa were married to their abusers, Patricia was divorced from her batterer, and Shannon had a son with the man she was convicted of killing. All of the women, except Elaine, who does not have children, have both raised families and worked outside the home prior to their incarceration.

Although the number of women I interviewed was relatively small, I do not feel that this in any way has limited the goals and findings of my research. I am not seeking a quantitative, statistical analysis of battered women's actions or experiences. Instead, I am interested in learning the about these experiences in depth, from the women themselves. As social theorists Barney Glaser and Anselm Strauss explain, in generating theory, "a single case can indicate a general conceptual category or property; a few more cases can confirm the indication."[12]

The interviews took place over a three-month period, from May to July 1993. Although two of the women had been moved to a minimum security prison, the other two remained at the maximum security institution where the Framingham Eight had originally formed. Because I had greater access to MCI Lancaster, the minimum security prison, I was able to visit the women there more frequently, meeting with each of them two or three times. This allowed us to build a more comfortable relationship, which considerably benefited the scope of the interviews. The total interviewing time for each woman ranged from two to three hours, depending on the access permitted by each institution. Often, we continued our conversations long after I had turned the recorder off, discussing their treatment in prison, their families, and other issues that were important to

---

[10] The group was formed by the women themselves in 1990. By the time I contacted these women in March of 1993, one woman, Meekah Scott, had been released from prison pending the appeal of her case in court. (Under Massachusetts clemency guidelines, a person may not appeal for clemency until he or she has exhausted all remedies within the state's judicial system.) Although this left only seven women appealing for clemency, the group retained its original name.

[11] I originally interviewed five women; however, one later declined to have her story published in this book.

[12] Barney G. Glaser and Anselm Strauss, *The Discovery of Grounded Theory* (Chicago: Aldine, 1967), 30.

them. In the course of writing this book, I have established friendships with several of these women and continue to correspond with them on a regular basis. I set forth my personal involvement to alert the reader of possible assumptions and biases which shape this text. I undertook this project with the hope that my discoveries would be able to make some contribution to these and other women's lives. I hope that I have been able to satisfy this goal, which, as sociologist Norman Denzin argues, should be established by any researcher in the social sciences:

> We must remember that our primary obligation is always to the people we study, not to our project or to a larger discipline. The lives and stories that we hear and study are given to us under a promise, that promise being that we protect those who have shared with us. And, in return, this sharing will allow us to write life documents that speak to the human dignity, the suffering, the hopes, the dreams, and the lives lost by the people we study.[13]

THE THEORY

I view domestic violence and these women's acts not through an individual, psychological perspective but from a larger, social interactionist position. I am not interested in analyzing whether or not these women, in taking their batterers' lives, were right or wrong; this work is not intended to serve as a legal determination of whether the women's actions were actually justified self-defense or not. Instead, I hope to discover how these women view themselves and their actions, and if the labels that the legal and psychiatric communities have applied to them seem to suitably describe their lives and experiences. As Norman Denzin notes: "Every human being . . . defines the world differently. If sociologists are to accurately explain these different definitions and relate them to action, they must penetrate the subjective world of concepts, experiences, and reactions."[14] Thus, in this study, the women's perspectives are as significant and meaningful as any "objective" reality. I am attempting to uncover their own reality and discover how, if at all, it has been altered by social forces, what these forces are, and if they have any implication for future work on behalf of battered women.

---

[13] Norman Denzin, *Interpretive Biography* (Newbury Park, CA: Sage Publications, 1989), 83. Reprinted with permission.
[14] Norman Denzin, *The Research Act: A Theoretical Introduction to Sociological Methods* (New Jersey: Prentice Hall, 1989), 183. Reprinted with permission.

In *The Research Act*, Norman Denzin describes the three basic principles that ground the symbolic interactionist perspective:

> First, social reality as it is sensed, known, and understood is a social production. Interacting individuals produce and define their own definitions of situations. Second, humans are assumed to be capable of engaging in "minded," self-reflective behavior. They are capable of shaping and guiding their own behavior and that of others. Thus, in the course of taking their own standpoint and fitting that standpoint to the behaviors of others, humans interact with one another. Interaction is seen as an emergent, negotiated, often unpredictable concern. Interaction is symbolic because it involves the manipulation of symbols, words, meaning, and languages.[15]

The definition of a situation is created by interacting individuals, using symbols and language which in turn affect both understanding and behavior.[16] Meaning is a collective process, a social action that involves relationships of power and control. I approached the stories of the Framingham Eight with this assumption: that the meanings of their past abuse and own behavior have been altered through interactions with others. I anticipated that labels and words, such as the battered woman syndrome, have revised the perceptions of these women's actions and produced a new social reality. But I have also attempted to examine whether the women are comfortable with these new definitions of the situation, and whether they feel these labels sufficiently describe their own experiences. For, as feminist theorist Shulamit Reinharz argues, "the concept of defining a situation implies that people have the ability to define and control. Studying women's lives (and the lives of other groups) reveals that women have little control over their lives and struggle continuously to gain some control."[17] How much control do these women, appealing for clemency on the grounds that they suffered from the battered woman syndrome, have

---

[15] Ibid., 5.

[16] Definitions of the situation, Shulamit Reinharz explains, play a significant role within symbolic interactionist theory: "Definitions of the situation are important because they produce the labels that are applied to acts and people and thus describe the social world that we produce and that in turn produces us." Shulamit Reinharz, "The Social Psychology of a Miscarriage: An Application of Symbolic Interaction Theory and Method," in *Women and Symbolic Interaction*, ed. Mary Jo Deegan and Michael Hill (Boston: Allen & Unwin, Inc., 1987), 230.

[17] Ibid., 247.

over their lives and the way their lives are interpreted by others? How have these new definitions of the situation — the battered woman syndrome, the cycle of violence, and learned helplessness — affected the women's understandings of their pasts? Are these accurate representations of their experiences? Will I find that, in accepting these definitions and stereotypes, there is a disjunction between the reality of these women's experiences and how society understands them?

Social disorganization occurs when the individual and society differ in their interpretation of behaviors and the definitions of situations. Although this disjunction can result in contradictions, it can also foster innovation and change as new perspectives and definitions emerge to resolve these conflicts. If such a disjunction does exist for these women, will it provide room for transformation and new, expanded definitions?

THE METHODOLOGY

I approached this project with a primary concern: I would not attempt to prove or disprove any set theory about battered women who kill their abusers, but I would allow the women themselves to help me generate a theory or set of theories to adequately describe their own experiences. Although I did, of course, bring to my research some general problems and hypotheses, I wanted to avoid placing these women and their stories into rigid categories that might ignore their variations and further silence their own voices. As I have stated, one of the primary purposes of my project has been to investigate whether the categories and theories currently used to describe these women are felt to be accurate and meaningful by the women themselves.

My perspective follows the grounded theory approach to data analysis, set forth by sociologists Barney Glaser and Anselm Strauss. The grounded theory method is based on the discovery or generation of theory from the data itself, rather than the verification of theory through the use of collected data.

> To be sure one goes out and studies an area with a particular sociological perspective, and with a focus, a general question, or a problem in mind. But he can (and we believe should) also study an area without any preconceived theory that dictates, prior to the research, "relevancies" in concepts and hypotheses. Indeed it is presumptuous to assume that one begins to know the

relevant categories and hypotheses until the "first days in the field," at least, are over.[18]

My procedure followed Glaser and Strauss' prescription. Although I approached my first interview with a general set of questions, I found myself reformulating my interview schedule and goals as I began to talk with a few of the women and gain a sense of the issues that seemed most important to them. It was in speaking with Elaine Hyde and Lisa Grimshaw, two of the first women I met, that I first questioned how their knowledge of the battered woman syndrome might have affected their perceptions of their abusers' deaths and of their own identities. I was struck by the comfort and familiarity with which they employed terms such as "battered woman syndrome" and "cycle of violence," and I wondered when and how they had learned these terms, and whether they felt this language had any true connection to what had happened in their lives.

Of the various methodologies I could have chosen to collect my data, that of interviewing seemed most useful to my project for several reasons. First, I felt strongly that I wanted to work directly with the women I was studying, to make contact with them, and to get to know the actual people behind these cases. Related to this was a desire to hear the women's stories from their own mouths, and to discover what their actions meant to them instead of what others (psychologists, lawyers, judges, and researchers such as myself) said they meant.

I used a specific type of interview in my research: the life story interview. The life story is an account that focuses on a particular period or event in a person's life. It differs from a life history in that it does not attempt to describe the totality of a life, but a segment of it. I chose the life story method because I was interested in learning about a specific period within these women's lives, beginning with the abuse they had suffered and ending with their appeals for clemency.

Both the life story and life history approach comprise what Norman Denzin terms the biographical method, "the studied use and collection of life-documents, or documents of life, which describe turning-point moments in individuals' lives."[19] These documents can range from autobiographies to court records, from letters to interviews. The moment in which each woman killed her abuser may be considered an epiphany, a turning-point within her life story. An epiphany is an experience, often a crisis, that fundamentally changes a person's understanding of his or her

---

[18] Glaser and Strauss, 33-4.
[19] Denzin, *Interpretive Biography*, 7.

life. "The meanings of these experiences," Denzin explains, "are always given retrospectively, as they are relived and re-experienced in the stories persons tell about what has happened to them."[20] These life stories continually undergo revision and reconstruction, as definitions of situations are altered through social interaction.

Although I sought to discover each woman's understanding of her own experiences, I wanted to avoid a mere collection of autobiographical accounts, however interesting they may be. Instead, my intention was to analyze the women's stories for commonalties or contradictions. In order to accomplish this, I employed a semi-structured interview format, and I recorded and transcribed each interview in its entirety. While I brought an identical set of written questions to each interview and was careful to cover the same themes and central questions with all of the women, I allowed for some flexibility in the process. My questions were generally open-ended, encouraging each woman to speak freely without interruption. Usually, however, I followed the open-ended questions with more specific inquiries to elucidate their responses. This open-ended, semi-structured interview format enabled the women to describe their experiences from their own perspectives, using their own meaningful terms, while allowing me to draw conclusions from their stories as a whole.

In addition to these personal interviews, I have relied on police and court records, newspaper accounts, statements from public officials, and the findings of other researchers to substantiate my theoretical claims. I have also carefully analyzed the commutation petitions of all the women I interviewed, reviewing these legal documents over a period of several months at the Advisory Board of Pardons in Boston. Primarily, I have used these petitions to gain a sense of how the women have presented their cases to the governor and Board of Pardons, and how they have described the actual incidents in which they killed their abusers.

It is important to remember that I am not attempting to determine the guilt or innocence of these women; I recognize that they must, in attempting to gain their release, place their actions within the context of the battered woman syndrome — their petitions rest on this very

---

[20] Ibid., 71. As Denzin explains, the life story is itself a product of symbolic interactionism; its construction is a social act. "No self or personal-experience story is ever an individual production. It derives from larger group, cultural, ideological, and historical contexts. . . . To understand a life, the epiphanies and the personal-experience and the self stories that represent and shape that life, one must penetrate and understand these larger structures. They provide the languages, emotions, taken-for-granted understandings and shared experiences from which the stories flow." Ibid., 73.

foundation. But, given this need to formally define their situations in these terms, my question remains: do these labels adequately represent their own experiences and perceptions? Are they accepting a new, yet equally limiting stereotype in exchange for freedom?

CHAPTER TWO

SELF-DEFENSE AND CLEMENCY: CLASSIFYING BATTERED WOMEN WHO KILL

> Woman herself recognizes that the world is masculine on the whole; those who fashioned it, ruled it, and still dominate it today are men. As for her, she does not consider herself responsible for it; it is understood that she is inferior and dependent; she has not learned the lessons of violence, she has never stood forth as subject before the other members of the group. Shut up in her flesh, her home, she sees herself as passive before these gods with human faces who set goals and establish values.
> – Simone De Beauvoir, *The Second Sex* [21]

Battered women who kill their abusers have traditionally, and unsuccessfully, attempted to place their actions within the legal precepts of self-defense. The battered woman syndrome was developed to describe the experiences of abused women so that others might judge their actions justifiable within a subjective framework of the self-defense requirements. Slowly gaining acceptance within the courts, the theory of the battered woman syndrome has also become an instrument for granting clemency to women convicted of killing their abusers.

---

[21] Simone De Beauvoir, *The Second Sex* (New York: Knopf, 1952), 664-5.

BATTERED WOMEN AND THE LAW

Until the late nineteenth century, marriage constituted ownership in common law, and a man could batter his wife with state sanction.[22] "By marriage," British jurist Sir William Blackstone wrote in 1768, "the husband and wife are one person in law: that is, the very being or legal existence of the woman is suspended."[23] When a husband wished to punish his wife, he was required by English common law only to follow the "rule of thumb:" he could beat her "with a stick as large as his finger but not larger than his thumb."[24] With this exception, laws in England and the United States have traditionally considered domestic abuse a private matter. In 1864, a North Carolina court gave this ruling in a case in which a man had choked his wife: "[T]he law permits him to use towards his wife such a degree of force, as is necessary to control an unruly temper, and make her behave herself . . . the law will not invade the domestic forum, or go behind the curtain. It prefers to leave the parties to themselves."[25]

In 1871, Alabama became the first state to deny a husband's right to batter his wife, remarking that the "wife had the right to the same protection of the law that the husband can invoke for himself."[26] However, this decision was largely symbolic: over the next century, non-intervention was the primary approach to crimes in the domestic sphere.

In the late 1960s, the women's movement brought attention to the problem of domestic violence in this country. Framing partner violence as a feminist issue, activists stressed that violence against women derived from the patriarchal and sexist values of American society.[27] They pointed to inequalities embedded within social and legal institutions that prevented

---

[22] Elizabeth Schneider, "Equal Rights to Trial for Women: Sex Bias in the Law of Self-Defense," *Harvard Civil Rights-Civil Liberties Law Review* 15.3 (1980): 626. See also Angela Browne, *When Battered Women Kill* (New York: The Free Press, 1987), 164-8, for further discussion of the legal history of wife abuse.

[23] William Blackstone, *Commentaries on the Laws of England*, as quoted in R. Emerson Dobash and Russell Dobash, *Violence against Wives: A Case against the Patriarchy* (New York: The Free Press, 1979), 60. "For as [the husband] is to answer for her misbehavior, the law thought it reasonable to intrust him with this power of chastisement, in the same moderation that a man is allowed to correct his apprentices or children. . . ." William Blackstone, *Commentaries on the Laws of England*, as quoted in U.S. Commission on Civil Rights, *Under the Rule of Thumb: Battered Women and the Administration of Justice* (Washington, D.C.: GPO, January 1982), 2.

[24] *Under the Rule of Thumb*, 2.

[25] *State v. Black*, 60 NC. 262, 1 Win. 266 (1864), as quoted in *Under the Rule of Thumb*, 2.

[26] *Fulgham v. State*, 46 Ala. 143 (1871)

[27] Gondolf and Fisher, 1.

women from achieving equal rights with men. For example, a woman could not obtain a restraining order against her violent husband unless she was willing to file for divorce at the same time.[28]

In the early 1970s, feminist and battered women activists helped establish the first battered women's shelters in this country. Growing interest in effective intervention for domestic violence in turn created a demand for research on the extent of the problem. In 1975, sociologist Murray Straus and colleagues conducted a nationwide study of family violence through in-person interviews with 2,000 couples. Their study found that at least one violent incident had occurred in 16 percent of these marriages during that year. Twenty-eight percent of the couples reported that there had been violence since the marriage began.[29] Eventually, the U.S. Department of Justice responded to these figures and calls from battered women's advocates by increasing funding between 1976 and 1981 for shelter services, batterer intervention programs, and tougher domestic violence prosecution policies.[30]

By 1980, 47 states had adopted legislation strengthening their criminal justice systems' response to domestic violence.[31] These statutes aimed to increase victims' rights and legal options, and to protect them from future violence by strengthening restraining orders against batterers. In 1984, the U.S. Attorney General's Task Force on Family Violence recommended that state and local police departments adopt policies supporting arrest in cases of spouse abuse.[32] By 1992, 14 states and the District of Columbia had instituted laws mandating arrest in domestic violence crimes.[33]

---

[28] Jeffrey Fagan, *The Criminalization of Domestic Violence: Promises and Limits*, National Institute of Justice Research Report (Washington, D.C., January 1996), 2-3.

[29] Murray A. Straus, Richard J. Gelles, and Suzanne K. Steinmetz, *Behind Closed Doors: Violence in the American Family* (New York: Anchor Press, 1980). The study used a national probability sample of 2,143 currently married or cohabitating couples, randomly divided between male and female participants.

[30] Fagan, 6-7.

[31] Ibid., 8. In 1975, the international police training manual still recommended that officers merely separate the parties and leave the scene of partner violence. The recommendations were revised in the mid-1980s to suggest that officers deal with violence in the home as they would treat assaults committed elsewhere. See Murray A. Strauss and Richard J. Gelles, "Societal Change in Family Violence from 1975 to 1985 as Revealed by Two National Surveys," in *Understanding Partner Violence: Prevalence, Causes, Consequences, & Solutions*, ed. Sandra M. Stith and Murray A. Straus (Minneapolis: National Council on Family Relations, 1995), 24.

[32] Ibid., 11

[33] Barbara J. Hart, "State Codes on Domestic Violence: Analysis, Commentary, and Recommendations," *Juvenile and Family Court Journal* 43 (1992): 4.

Yet, despite these significant policy and legislative changes, residues of domestic violence's legal past remain evident today. Rates of family violence are still alarmingly high.

Studies estimate that between 21 percent and 34 percent of all adult women will experience violence from a male partner.[34] In 1992, about 27 percent of all violence against women was committed by a current or former spouse or boyfriend. About one in five female victims of partner violence reported that they had experienced at least three similar assaults within the past year.[35] In addition, the federal government estimates that between 18 and 30 percent of all women visiting emergency rooms are there for injuries inflicted by a partner or spouse.[36]

Frequently, domestic violence results in the death of a woman. Statistics published by the Department of Justice reveal that over 30 percent of all female homicide victims are murdered by their partners.[37] According to the FBI, between 1976 and 1996, 31,260 women were victims of intimate murder. Sixty-four percent of these women were killed by their husbands, five percent by their ex-husbands, and 31 percent by their boyfriends or non-marital partners.[38]

WHEN A WOMAN KILLS

While violence against a woman has been historically sanctioned, the injury of a man at the hands of his wife has always been condemned. As Sir William Blackstone noted in 1786, a wife's killing of her husband amounted to an act of treason against the state:

---

[34] Mary P. Koss et al., *No Safe Haven: Male Violence against Women at Home, at Work, and in the Community* (Washington, D.C.: The American Psychological Association, 1994), 42.

[35] Department of Justice, Bureau of Justice Statistics, *Violence Between Intimates: Domestic Violence* (Washington, D.C., November 1994, NCJ 149259). Source: The National Crime Victimization Survey, 1987-1992.

[36] According to national statistics, female victims of intimate violence suffer medical expenses and other costs totaling about 150 million dollars annually. Department of Justice, Bureau of Justice Statistics, *Violence by Intimates: Analysis of Data on Crimes by Current or Former Spouses, Boyfriends, and Girlfriends* (Washington, D.C., March 1998, NCJ 167237).

[37] Department of Justice, *Violence by Intimates*. Source: FBI, Supplementary Homicide Reports (SHR), 1976-1996. Intimates or partners generally include current or former spouses, same sex partners, boyfriends, and girlfriends. Murder includes nonnegligent manslaughter.

[38] Department of Justice, *Violence by Intimates*. Source: FBI, Supplementary Homicide Reports (SHR), 1976-1996.

> Husband and Wife, in the language of the law, are styled baron and feme. . . . [I]f the baron kills his feme it is the same as if he had killed a stranger, or any other person; but if the feme kills her baron, it is regarded by the laws as a much more atrocious crime as she not only breaks through the restraints of humanity and conjugal affection, but throws off all subjection to the authority of her husband. And therefore the law denominates her crime a species of treason, and condemns her to the same punishment as if she had killed the king.[39]

Even today, when a battered woman not only fights back, but actually kills her abuser, she radically challenges gender-biased views. Her act questions society's perception of the family as a sacred institution providing comfort and support, and the theory of female helplessness in the face of male power and control. As feminist legal scholar Cynthia Gillespie explains: "If the exercise of merely defensive force challenges traditional views of appropriate female conduct, the use of deadly force by a woman against a man who has abused her must contradict social stereotypes and threaten a basic conception of traditional society."[40] As a result, women have historically faced harsher penalties than men who kill their lovers or spouses. Statistics show that more women than men have been charged with first- or second-degree murder for killing a partner. In addition, a woman, if convicted of this type of killing, would often receive a longer prison sentence than a man convicted of the same crime.[41]

What is striking is that when women do kill, it is often in their own defense.[42] The vast majority of these homicides take place within the

---

[39] William Blackstone, *Commentaries on the Laws of England*, as quoted in Dobash and Dobash, 59.

[40] Gillespie, 629.

[41] "Abusive men who kill their partners serve an average of two-to-six year terms. Women who kill their partners, usually in self-defense, serve an average of fifteen years," National Coalition against Domestic Violence, "National Estimates and Facts about Domestic Abuse," *NCADV Voice* (Winter 1989): 12. In addition, the proportion of female inmates convicted of partner violence who received life terms or the death penalty (33 percent) is higher than that for male prisoners (19 percent) in this country. Department of Justice, *Violence Between Intimates*. Source: Survey of Inmates in State Correctional Facilities, 1991.

[42] "Self-defense is involved approximately seven times more frequently when women kill men than when men kill women. The various studies are consistent in showing that victim precipitation occurs significantly more often when a man is killed by a woman then when a woman is killed by a man. Thus, when women kill, they are far more likely than men to be

context of intimate relationships marked by severe physical and mental abuse.[43] A national study of 1988 homicide cases revealed that in 44 percent of wife defendant cases, there was evidence that the husband had assaulted his wife at the time of the killing. In contrast, there was evidence in only 10 percent of the husband defendant cases that the wife's violence had provoked the homicide.[44] Another survey found that about one-third of all women convicted of homicide had killed a lover or spouse; 72 percent of these women had no prior arrests.[45]

Ironically, as I found in my own research, the police and the courts have been quick to intervene when women fight back. As psychologist Angela Browne notes in her study of battered women who killed, "the same system that failed to protect them from their partners' violence immediately arrested and prosecuted them when they responded in their own defense."[46] Once within the criminal justice system, these women are faced with the legal institutionalization of the sex-biases that opposed them in greater society; they find that the law of self-defense discriminates against women in general, and battered women in particular.

SELF-DEFENSE

In her book *Justifiable Homicide*, Cynthia Gillespie describes why women have difficulty claiming self-defense when they kill their abusers. "The problem appears to result from a combination of two things; first,

---

responding to, rather than initiating, violence." Jacquelyn Campbell, *Nursing Assessment for Risk of Homicide with Battered Women* (Aspen: Aspen Publishers, 1986), 37. Statistics also show that historically, the rate of women committing homicide has remained stable; women perpetrate about 15 percent of the homicides in the United States. Department of Justice, Federal Bureau of Investigation, *Uniform Crime Reports for 1983* (Washington, D.C., 1984).

[43] Walker, *The Battered Woman*, 38. The majority of battered women who kill use a household utensil or the batterer's gun to commit the act. Coramae Mann, "Getting Even? Women Who Kill in Domestic Encounters," in *Representing . . . Battered Women Who Kill*, ed. Sara Lee Johann and Frank Osanka (Springfield: Charles C. Thomas, 1989), 12-9. See also Browne, *When Battered Women Kill*, 140, and Walker, *The Battered Woman Syndrome*, 40.

[44] The defendants in these cases included common-law and separated spouses, but not divorced couples. U. S. Department of Justice, Bureau of Justice Statistics, *Spouse Murder Defendants in Large Urban Counties*, Executive Summary (Washington, D.C., September 1995, NCJ-156831), 2.

[45] Department of Justice, *Violence Between Intimates*. Source: Survey of Inmates in State Correctional Facilities, 1991.

[46] Browne, *When Battered Women Kill*, 159.

the law itself, which over many centuries has come to embody masculine assumptions about the circumstances that entitle a person to act in self-defense; and second, our society's ambivalent and biased attitudes about women and its acceptance of violence against them."[47]

Self-defense law rests on the view that a person may take reasonable action to defend him or herself from serious physical harm. The law of self-defense states that "one who is not the aggressor in an encounter is justified in using a reasonable amount of force against his adversary when he reasonably believes (a) that he is in immediate danger of unlawful bodily harm from his adversary and (b) that the use of such force is necessary to avoid this danger."[48]

A successful self-defense claim relies on the determination that the defendant's actions were justifiable; as I will show, the dichotomy between justification and excuse is particularly relevant to the cases of battered women who kill. Essentially, self-defense as justification focuses on the act itself. It entails finding that the action was correct given its circumstances; any person in the same situation would be justified in using defensive force. In contrast, a judgment of excuse focuses on the actor; it concludes that the act, though wrong, should be tolerated because of the actor's state of mind. An impaired mental state or insanity defense would be examples of excuse.[49] The law looks at excuse only after justification fails. In other words, if a jury determines that the circumstances of an act claimed to be in self-defense do not justify the act, then the jury looks to excuse and examines the defendant's mental state. The implications of a justification or an excuse finding are important; though both may result in a verdict of not guilty, justified action is deemed universally appropriate, while excuse suggests that the act was personal to the defendant and should not be publicly encouraged.[50]

In order for jurors to determine whether or not an act constitutes justifiable self-defense, they must evaluate its reasonableness. Several legal rules must be met for a person's claim to be deemed reasonable within the

---

[47] Gillespie, xi.
[48] Wayne R. LaFave and Austin W. Scott, Jr., *Criminal Law*, 2nd ed. (St. Paul, MN: The West Publishing Company, 1986), 454. Reprinted with permission.
[49] See Elizabeth Schneider, "Describing and Changing: Women's Self-Defense Work and the Problem of Expert Testimony on Battering," in *Representing . . . Battered Women Who Kill*, ed. Sara Lee Johann and Frank Osanka (Springfield: Charles C. Thomas, 1989), 85.
[50] See Steven D. Nuttal, "An Essay on the Criminal Law Justification Defense" (diss., Ohio State University, 1991), 3. In addition, while an excuse finding may lead to an acquittal in court, the defendant may still lose his or her freedom if committed to a mental institution.

criminal justice system.[51] The first is the equal force rule, which states that a person may only use armed force when facing an adversary who is also using unlawful armed force.[52] The law also includes an immediacy requirement; the danger to the victim of the attack must be viewed as imminent to justify self-defense.[53] The final element incorporated into the law is the duty to retreat; the victim must seek any avenue of escape from the attacker before using deadly force.

→ The equal force rule discriminates against battered women because it is based on the assumption that the adversaries in any encounter are men. It fails to allow for a confrontation between a man and a woman who differ in size and strength. Women are not trained in the use of violence nor taught to use their bodies as men are. Men are raised to be fighters; aggression and strength are valued and held as ideal male qualities, while femininity is seen as embodying passivity and frailty. Even unarmed, a man can usually overpower and injure a woman much more easily than she can harm him; the fists of a man have been proven deadly weapons in many domestic violence cases. Thus, it is not surprising that a woman might use a weapon against an unarmed male attacker. But, in so doing, she may fail to satisfy the rigid equal force requirement of self-defense.

→ The imminent danger rule also rejects the situation in which many battered women kill their abusers. Imminency presupposes a one-time adversarial encounter between two (male) strangers, not a prolonged period of abuse at the hands of a lover or spouse. This rule, in focusing solely on the immediate circumstances of the killing, fails to acknowledge the significance of past violence or the threat of future assaults. Battered women often kill their abusers after an attack; to an outside observer, any

---

[51] Self-defense law generally requires "that the defendant's belief in the necessity of using force to prevent harm to himself is a reasonable one, so that one who honestly though unreasonably believes in the necessity of using force in self-protection loses the defense. When his belief is reasonable, however, he may be mistaken in his belief and still have the defense. Thus one may be justified in shooting to death an adversary who, having threatened to kill him, reaches for his pocket as if for a gun, though it later appears that he had no gun and was only reaching for his handkerchief." LaFave and Scott, 457.

[52] Deadly force may justifiably be used in self-defense only when one reasonably believes that an assailant is about to inflict serious physical injury or death, and that deadly force is necessary to prevent it. Generally, "this precludes the use of a deadly weapon against an *unarmed* assailant." Ibid., 456.

[53] "Case law and legislation concerning self-defense require that the defendant reasonably believe his adversary's violence to be almost immediately forthcoming . . . As a general matter, the requirement that the attack reasonably appear to be imminent is a sensible one. If the threatened violence is scheduled to arrive in the more distant future, there may be other avenues open to the defendant to prevent it other than to kill or injure the prospective attacker; but this is not so where the attack is imminent." Ibid., 458.

immediate danger may seem to have passed. As feminist legal scholar Elizabeth Schneider explains, "Homicides committed by women frequently occur with a time lag, while the man is asleep or while his back is turned. Typically, the man beats the woman, sometimes threatening to kill her, until he passes out or falls asleep. Fearing that when he wakes he will beat her more severely or act on his threat, she attacks him while he sleeps."[54] Without knowledge of past threats or abuse, juries may ask how a sleeping man could pose an imminent danger to a woman.[55] Forced by this rule to evaluate only the immediate circumstances of an incident, juries seldom receive enough evidence to judge whether a battered woman's action was reasonably justified.

The final obstacle to a battered woman's claim of self-defense is the requirement to retreat from a life-threatening attack. This issue goes to the heart of the misconceptions concerning domestic abuse. Confronted with this requirement, juries ask: "Why didn't the woman simply leave the abusive relationship in the first place? In the face of danger, why didn't she retreat?"[56] Once again, the law assumes that the attack occurs between two strangers on the street, not in the context of an intimate relationship. Although the retreat requirement varies across jurisdictions, in domestic disputes, the defender generally must retreat when the aggressor is the co-occupant of the home where the attack is taking place.[57] According to this rule, a woman is obligated to abandon her own children, house, and often, all financial security if she is threatened. If she fails to do so, a jury may find her behavior unreasonable.

The law purports to rely on an objective standard of reasonableness. However, this apparent neutrality of the self-defense requirements is deceptive. Reasonableness is determined by society's standards, a society in which women have traditionally been cast as unreasonable and irrational. "Our understandings of what is objective have been based largely on male experience," Elizabeth Schneider argues, "and stereotypes of men as

---

[54] Schneider, "Equal Rights," 634. Reprinted with permission.

[55] In *People v. Garcia*, a woman successfully claimed self-defense in killing an abuser several hours after she had actually been attacked. Inez Garcia had been raped by two men who told her that they would come back to harm her. When one of the men returned later and drew a knife on her, she shot and killed him. The court's ruling extended the imminent danger requirement beyond the period immediately prior to the assault. See *People v. Garcia*, Cr. No. 4259 (Superior Court, Monterey County, Cal., 1977).

[56] Most jurisdictions do exempt people who are attacked in their own homes from this requirement. While Massachusetts does not require a person to retreat from an attacker who has *unlawfully* entered the house, it does require retreat from an attack by a co-occupant. Mass. Gen. L. ch. 278, sect. 8A. This obviously poses a problem for battered women who are usually threatened by people with whom they live.

[57] LaFave and Scott, 461.

objective and analytical have also been contrasted with stereotypes of women as subjective and emotional."[58] What seems to be a neutral, objective determination of reasonableness is actually a *reasonable man's* standard, formed around the gender-biased attitudes of those who have fashioned the law; there is never any mention of the reasonable woman.[59] Cynthia Gillespie describes this fundamental hurdle a woman faces when attempting to prove the rationality of her actions in response to an assault:

> A woman — who has spent 20, or 30, or 50 years absorbing the message that she is, and ought to be, gentle and weak and helpless... that she cannot really rely on her own strength to save herself from danger; that male violence is profoundly to be feared but cannot be defended against — is bound to view a violent assault differently than would a man whose own training in these matters is likely to have been so very different. A response to violence that might be unreasonable in a strong, healthy, "real" man may be perfectly reasonable in a woman.[60]

Partly because of this biased standard of reasonableness, battered women who kill often claim insanity, rather than self-defense; courts and jurors, as a reflection of society as a whole, have been more willing to view women as irrational and mentally unstable than reasonably justified in their actions.

Gradually, however, some jurisdictions have begun to recognize the inadequacy of this objective approach to self-defense cases. In the landmark 1977 case of *State v. Wanrow*, a woman shot a man whom she believed to be a child molester when he entered her home.[61] The Washington Supreme Court set a major legal precedent by asserting that this woman may have been justified in using armed force against her unarmed male attacker. The Court acknowledged that the physical inequalities that exist between the sexes may affect a woman's perception of what constitutes the amount of force necessary to defend herself from a man's attack. The jury, the Court ruled, must consider the full circumstances of the woman's act and the potential need for a woman to

---

[58] Schneider, "Describing and Changing," 93. Reprinted with permission.
[59] See Schneider, "Equal Rights," 635-6.
[60] Gillespie, 629.
[61] *State v. Wanrow* 88 Wash. 2d 221 (Wash. 1977). Although not a "battered woman" case, Wanrow laid a foundation for the use of a subjective standard of reasonableness and the admission of expert testimony on the battered woman syndrome.

use a weapon against an unarmed male assailant. The Court made this significant statement: "In our society women suffer from a conspicuous lack of training in and the means of developing those skills necessary to effectively repel a male assailant without resorting to the use of deadly weapons."[62]

In *Wanrow*, the Court also acknowledged that an objective standard of reasonableness may fail to account for the experiences and perceptions of women as both individuals and members of an historically oppressed group:

> The respondent was entitled to have the jury *consider her actions in the light of her own perceptions of the situation, including those perceptions which were the product of our nation's long and unfortunate history of sex discrimination.* Until such time as the effects of that history are eradicated, care must be taken to assure that our self-defense instructions afford women the right to have their conduct judged in light of the individual physical handicaps which are the product of sex discrimination. To fail to do so is to deny the right of the individual woman involved to trial by the same rules which are applicable to male defendants. (Italics added)[63]

Encouraged by this initial acceptance of a subjective standard of reasonableness, advocates and attorneys introduced a theory describing the particular perceptions of battered women in cases of self-defense. This theory was the battered woman syndrome.

In 1984, the case of *State v. Kelly* set a precedent for the admission of expert testimony on the battered woman syndrome in cases of battered women who kill their abusers.[64] Gladys Kelly had been abused by her

---

[62] Ibid.

[63] Ibid.

[64] *State v. Kelly*, 97 N.J. 178, 478 A.2d 364 (N.J. 1984). In *Ibn-Tamas v. U.S.*, Lenore Walker became the first psychologist to serve as an expert witness for battered women defendants; however, the judge excluded her testimony because the methodology used in "the expert's study of battered women" was not generally accepted in her field. *Ibn Tamas v. U.S.* 407 A.2d 626 (D. C. 1979). The rules for the admissibility of expert testimony varied across jurisdictions, but most states traditionally relied on the *Dyas* test. The basic requirements were that testimony offered must be beyond the knowledge of the average person, the witness "must have sufficient skill or expertise in the field to make it appear that his opinion ... will aid the trier in the search for the truth," and "the state of the pertinent art of scientific knowledge must permit a reasonable opinion to be asserted by an expert." *Dyas v. United States*, 376 A.2d 827 (D.C. 1977). (Walker's testimony in *Ibn-Tamas* was excluded based on the third *Dyas* criterion). The more liberal Rule 702 of the

husband throughout their marriage. On the day of the homicide, her husband had been drinking and began beating her in public. During the fight that ensued, Ms. Kelly stabbed him with a pair of scissors. She was charged with second-degree murder of her husband. The New Jersey Supreme Court recognized that Mrs. Kelly's history of abuse may have had a great impact on her state of mind when she killed her husband, and that testimony on the battered woman syndrome was relevant to her claim of self-defense and should therefore be admitted.

Although the court admitted testimony on the battered woman syndrome in *Kelly,* judges and attorneys throughout the United States frequently ruled similar testimony inadmissible over the next several years. Many battered women were not able to meet the standards of self-defense law; they were encouraged to plead guilty before trial, or they were convicted by juries adhering to these rigid requirements established by the criminal justice system. As a result, women who killed their abusers were frequently found guilty of murder or manslaughter; they often received sentences ranging from eight to fifteen years, and sometimes life in prison.[65] These women were tried during a time when domestic violence had not yet been "discovered" by society, when the theory of the battered

---

Federal Rules of Evidence has now been adopted nationally, allowing for greater admissibility of expert testimony on the battered woman syndrome. Rule 702 states that testimony is admissible even if the jury has general knowledge of the subject, as long as the testimony will aid the jury's understanding of the factual issues of the case. For a discussion of admissibility trends among the states, see the Epilogue; Janet Parrish, "Trend Analysis: Expert Testimony on Battering and Its Effects in Criminal Cases," in *The Validity and Use of Evidence Concerning Battering and Its Effects in Criminal Trials,* Report Responding to Section 40507 of the Violence Against Women Act (Washington, D.C.: U.S. Department of Justice and U.S. Department of Health and Human Services, May 1996, NCJ 160972); and Cynthia L. Coffee, "A Trend Emerges: A State Survey on the Admissibility of Expert Testimony Concerning the Battered Woman Syndrome," *Journal of Family Law* 25 (1986-7): 374. For further discussion of *Ibn-Tamas v. United States,* see Meredith Cross, "The Expert as Educator: A Proposed Approach to the Use of Battered Woman Syndrome Expert Testimony" *Vanderbilt Law Review* 35 (1982): 749; Coffee, 392; and Schneider, "Equal Rights," 646.

[65] In most states, there are two degrees of murder. First degree murder includes an intent to kill, accompanied by premeditation and reflection before the act. Second degree murder may be an intent to kill that is not premeditated or deliberated before the act. Manslaughter consists of an intentional killing committed under extenuating circumstances, such as heat-of-passion or provocation. "While a reasonable belief in the existence of circumstances requiring the use of deadly force is necessary for complete exoneration under an affirmative defense such as self-defense, there is some authority that an 'imperfect' defense (in the sense that the belief was not reasonable) will downgrade what would otherwise be murder to voluntary manslaughter." LaFave and Scott, 371-2. Battered women are often convicted of voluntary manslaughter, rather than murder, based on a provocation argument.

woman syndrome was either unknown or unaccepted; they remained incarcerated because their actions were viewed through the lens of the past.

However, in recent years, courts and politicians have begun to judge these women's actions through the new lens of the battered woman syndrome. As a result, many battered women have stepped forward requesting clemency. They have been given the chance to tell their stories again, stories that may have changed in both their eyes and the eyes of the society that originally convicted them.

CLEMENCY

In September 1991, Governor William Weld of Massachusetts altered his state's commutation guidelines to include a new category for battered women who had killed their abusers. He established a uniform policy creating specific grounds on which a convict could seek commutation of her sentence. Under these guidelines, a petitioner could apply for commutation if she could demonstrate that: "further incarceration would constitute gross unfairness because of the basic inequities involved including . . . (iii) a history of abuse suffered by the petitioner at the hands of the victim which significantly contributed to or brought about the offense."[66]

Although Weld was not the first governor to consider granting clemency to battered women who killed their abusers, his formal alteration of the statutory guidelines marked a national precedent.[67] Essentially, Weld created a new commutation category, based on a theory developed to explain the behavior of battered women. Though the phrase was not explicitly used in the new guidelines, Weld himself stated that he would now "consider commutation petitions focusing on the battered woman

---

[66] Massachusetts, Executive Department, "Commutation Guidelines and Petition," issued by Governor William Weld, September, 1991: 1-2. Clause (iii) is Governor Weld's only addition to these guidelines. The Governor and his office view this alteration "as an opportunity for further consideration of these offenses, in terms of what we now know about how battering affects victims, both in their behavior and perceptions." Bob Cordy, interview with author, Boston, MA, 21 June 1993. Mr. Cordy served as legal counsel to Governor Weld.

[67] In 1990, Ohio Governor Richard Celeste commuted the sentences of twenty-five battered women convicted of killing or assaulting their abusers, based on their "profound and terrifying experience of being victims of physical and psychological violence and intimidation." As quoted in Daniel Kobil, "The Quality of Mercy Strained," *Texas Law Review* 69 (1991): 630. Reprinted with permission. Following Governor Celeste, Governor Schaefer of Maryland commuted the prison sentences of eight battered women. Neither of these states had specific commutation guidelines; the extension of clemency was at the sole discretion of the governors.

syndrome."[68] Massachusetts Lieutenant Governor Paul Cellucci elaborated: "One of the things we will be looking for in these petitions for commutation is the extent to which the battered woman syndrome defense was excluded" at trial. In many cases, that defense "wasn't even considered. If, in fact, it had been presented to a jury, the outcome of the case might well have been different."[69] The possibility of commutation was significant for both currently incarcerated women and those yet to enter the trial system. Governor Weld's action formally acknowledged the battered woman syndrome as a new category in which to place these women's experiences, perceptions, and acts of killing.

In February, 1992, the Massachusetts Domestic Violence Council submitted a petition to the Board of Pardons and Governor Weld, requesting the commutation of the Framingham Eight's sentences.[70] Their appeals were based on the claim that they suffered from the battered woman syndrome when they killed their abusers, and that the legal system failed to acknowledge the link between their history of abuse and the homicide itself. The petition stated:

> At each stage of the woman's "progress" through the trial system — pre-trial, trial, and post-trial — the legal system can and often does fail to recognize and reconcile the relationship between the batterer's abuse and the woman's actions. As a result, current law may be applied unfairly to battered women. Although the Board's role is not to sit as an appellate court, in deciding whether to grant commutation, it should take into account the obstacles that battered women face throughout the legal process.[71]

---

[68] As quoted in Toni Locy, "Weld Backs Commutation for Four Inmates: One Says Man She Killed Was Her Batterer," *The Boston Globe*, 21 January 1993, 29.

[69] Toni Locy, "Weld Urged to Free Eight Women: Commutations Sought for Inmates Who Killed Alleged Abusers," *The Boston Globe*, 15 February 1992, 15. Grants of commutation in other states have also been based on prior inadmissibility of the battered woman syndrome. In granting clemency to the 25 women in 1990, Governor Celeste noted that they "had been deprived of the chance to make a good case of self-defense because testimony on battered women's syndrome had not been allowed." Tamar Lewin, "More States Study Clemency for Women Who Killed Abusers," *The New York Times*, 21 February 1991, A19.

[70] The Domestic Violence Council consists of members of Massachusetts law firms, law schools, battered women's shelters, and other legal service providers.

[71] Domestic Violence Council, "Brief in Support of Petitions for Commutation (In the Matter of Commutation Petitions of Patricia Allen, Shannon Booker, Lisa Grimshaw,

Several of these eight women never went to trial at all; they pleaded guilty to charges out of their own fear or the ignorance of defense attorneys who felt that their stories of abuse were unrelated to their actions. Other women went to trial and were informed by judges that evidence relating to the battered woman syndrome was inadmissible, or that their claims of self-defense would not be heard. Although one was able to tell her story with the support of the battered woman syndrome, she was nevertheless convicted by a jury who felt that her actions still did not meet the traditional rules of self-defense.[72] In February, 1992, these women requested a review of their cases by the Governor, who alone could free them with a formal acknowledgment that society now viewed their actions in a new light.

MERCY OR EQUITY?

Clemency is one of the oldest institutions within our system of justice.[73] From the time of ancient Athens, rulers have extended mercy to those convicted of crimes in order to maintain peace within the social order.[74] Clemency is an extra-judicial exercise of power; it may be granted at the discretion of a ruler, but only when a convict has exhausted all other avenues of judicial recourse. Acts of clemency may be founded on one of two grounds: by remitting punishment, the executive ruler of a state or

---

Patricia Hennessy, Elaine Hyde, Eugenia Moore, Deborah Reid, and Meekah Scott)," Boston, MA: 19 February 1992, 21-2.

[72] Lisa Grimshaw was the first woman in Massachusetts to use the battered woman syndrome within the courts. Although her sentence was reduced from murder to manslaughter, she received the maximum penalty, 15 to 20 years, for her role in her husband's death.

[73] Legal scholar Daniel Kobil has written at length on the role of clemency within society: "The institution of clemency represents our oldest existing procedure for the remission of punishment. The universality of clemency and the failure of this hoary relic to become obsolete in any culture in which it has existed, not withstanding a long history of abuses, testifies to its usefulness." Kobil, "The Quality of Mercy Strained," 638.

[74] Ibid., 571. In English Law, the King traditionally wielded the pardoning power, but this right was eventually transferred to the colonial governors. Legal scholar Carla Johnson describes the way in which clemency came to have a place in American law: "Those developing the Federal Constitution agreed there was both room and need for a pardoning power in a democracy. Alexander Hamilton defended the inclusion of a pardoning power on the grounds that such a power is 'required by considerations of justice, humanity, and public policy.'" Carla Ann Johnson, "Entitled to Clemency: Mercy in the Criminal Law," *Law and Philosophy* 10 (1991): 114.

country can either perform a gesture of compassion or remedy injustices that have occurred within the legal system.[75]

As an act of mercy, clemency is strongly linked to compassion as defined outside the law. Legal mercy is the final hope for the convicted. While the untried place their fate in the due process of law, and those who are wrongly convicted may appeal their sentences to higher authorities, those who have exhausted all legal avenues must rely on mercy for their freedom. Clemency, in this case, is for one who asks forgiveness, who requests aid in a time of need, who supplicants himself or herself before a ruler who is empowered to give that assistance. After all, as legal theorist Carla Ann Johnson explains, "mercy is a response to another's great need, given despite the recipient's lack of an effective claim to it."[76]

But clemency may also be an instrument of equity, a gesture correcting past wrongs. Clemency has become a necessary component of a criminal justice system that occasionally creates injustices rather than remedies them. As legal scholar Daniel Kobil explains, "the extra-judicial correction of clemency provides a safety valve for our criminal justice system, another opportunity for an offender to tell her story more thoroughly, or at least differently, than she could at trial."[77] When viewed in this light, the granting of clemency has a paradoxical nature; essentially, it relies on the suspension of justice to achieve justice.

Two types of clemency are generally exercised within the United States: pardon and commutation. A pardon is equivalent to complete exoneration; it is a statement that a person is not guilty of the crime for which he or she was convicted. According to a decision of the United States Supreme Court, a pardon releases a person from both punishment and moral culpability "so that in the eyes of the law she is innocent as if she had never been charged or convicted."[78]

Commutation, the form of clemency offered to these eight Massachusetts women, is more limited than a pardon. It is essentially "the substitution of a milder punishment for one imposed by the court," Daniel Kobil explains. "Unlike a pardon, commutation in no way relieves the offender of the legal consequences of an offense, nor, presumably of moral guilt."[79] Generally, commutation results in the reduction of a sentence to the period of time a prisoner has already served. It is important to note that an executive's role in commuting a sentence is not equivalent to that

---

[75] Kobil, "The Quality of Mercy Strained," 571.
[76] Johnson, 117.
[77] Kobil, "The Quality of Mercy Strained," 613.
[78] *Schick v. Reed*, 419 U.S. 256, 273 n.8 (1974) as cited in Kobil, "The Quality of Mercy Strained," 576.
[79] Ibid., 577.

of an appellate court. The commutation of a prison sentence is merely an acknowledgment of unjust punishment in light of mitigating circumstances, such as terminal illness, or in the case of battered women, a history of abuse. Commutation is not equivalent to acquittal before the law on the grounds of self-defense.[80]

Procedures for granting commutations vary from state to state. Most states place the clemency power directly in the hands of the governor, while others give some power to an administrative board as well.[81] States also differ in the degree of specificity within their clemency guidelines. In some states, for example, the governor or administrative board has complete discretion as to which cases may be eligible for clemency; in other states strict guidelines must be followed.[82] In Massachusetts, the clemency power is invested in the State Advisory Board of Pardons, which makes a recommendation to the governor; the governor then makes the final judgment regarding each commutation. However, in Massachusetts, both the Board and the governor must follow specific guidelines setting forth the grounds on which an incarcerated person may be freed.[83]

Although both a pardon and a commutation can create physical freedom for the convicted, the difference between the two, like that between justification and excuse within the law of self-defense, may have significant implications for battered women who kill their abusers. I suggest that a parallel exists between the extra-judicial act of pardon and the justification of an action within the law of self-defense. Both essentially

---

[80] Commutation deals with the issue of punishment. "It addresses the incarceration, not the exoneration, of a person. The act of commutation is not a substitution for a jury's judgment. It does not address the guilt or innocence of a person." Bob Cordy, interview by author, Boston, MA, 21 June 1993.

[81] Twenty-nine states give the governor sole power to deliver grants of clemency. Sixteen states, including Massachusetts, give the clemency power to the governor and an advisory administrative board, which must have a majority vote in the affirmative in order for clemency to be granted. Five states place the clemency power in a governor-appointed administrative board alone. Kobil, "The Quality of Mercy Strained," 605.

[82] Only a few states actually have statutory standards that regulate the granting of clemency. Partly because of the widespread absence of guidelines, rates of granting clemency vary across states and among gubernatorial administrations. For further discussion of clemency procedures, see Kobil, "The Quality of Mercy Strained," 605, and Kobil, "Do the Paperwork or Die: Clemency, Ohio Style?" *Ohio State Law Journal* 52.3 (1991): 671.

[83] In Massachusetts, any petition for commutation must follow a series of steps before reaching the governor's desk: the petitioner must first have a hearing before the Parole Board, who makes a recommendation for or against commutation. If the petition is approved by a majority of the Board, the Governor's Council then reviews the petition, which, if approved by the Council, is finally placed before the governor for ratification

result in a determination of innocence and an exoneration of guilt. The equivalent of a commutation, however, would seem to lie in a judgment of excuse. And, as the law of self-defense demonstrates, an excuse-based judgment declares that an action is wrong but should be tolerated on the basis of the actor's mental state. Commutation, like excuse, again focuses on the qualities of the individual actor, stating that his or her behavior was unjustified and should not be universally encouraged. A commutation does not imply the innocence of the actor, but merely the unjust nature of the punishment.

This has important implications for women convicted of killing their abusers: Do these women believe that they deserved to be punished, but that they were unjustly sentenced? Or do they feel that their actions were justified, and that they should have been acquitted before a court of law? If they believe that they acted reasonably, should they be satisfied with a mere reduction of their sentences? I suggest that a tension exists between a claim of justified self-defense and a commutation, a contradiction that may be traced to the problems inherent in the foundation for these women's appeals: the battered woman syndrome.

CHAPTER 3

THE BATTERED WOMAN SYNDROME: CHALLENGES TO THE THEORY

Lenore Walker developed the theory of the battered woman syndrome to describe the psychological and behavioral reactions she observed among women abused within intimate relationships. Since its conception, this theory has served as a foundation for all subsequent work within the field of domestic violence. Judges have increasingly admitted expert testimony on the battered woman syndrome in self-defense cases, and clemency appeals by incarcerated battered women are now routinely based on this theory. Yet, although expert testimony on the battered woman syndrome has led to the acquittal of many women charged with murder, critics argue that the gains come at substantial cost: the syndrome may rely on and help perpetuate stereotypes of women as helpless or even insane. They suggest that the syndrome's terminology and theoretical constructs, particularly the concept of learned helplessness, may be inadequate and potentially damaging for the legal future of battered women defendants.

This chapter begins by introducing Walker's definition of a battered woman and the debate her category has engendered among feminist scholars. In the second part of the chapter, I describe the elements of the battered woman syndrome and criticisms this theory has received from the feminist legal community. Although various scholars have challenged aspects of the battered woman syndrome, I present the work of Martha Mahoney and Elizabeth Schneider as representative of the feminist legal critique. I have chosen these scholars because their comprehensive and cogent analyses have laid the foundation for ongoing legal research, writing, and advocacy in the field of domestic violence. These theorists note the ways in which the criminal justice system and the general public have misinterpreted the battered woman syndrome. However, they simply argue for the theory's careful use, not its complete elimination from a courtroom or clemency proceeding. Theorists do note that the syndrome, in focusing on the psychology of battered women, ignores other crucial aspects of their situations. Nonetheless, most scholars, including Mahoney and Schneider, stop short of proposing a complete alternative. The battered woman syndrome is valuable, they contend, as long as it is accompanied by a fuller description of battered women's experiences.

My research suggests, however, that the battered woman syndrome is fatally flawed, for its notion of learned helplessness — that women remain in abusive relationships because they are incapable of leaving — seems inaccurate.

The evidence upon which I am basing my conclusions will be presented fully in the next chapter, where I explore the specific cases of four women who killed their batterers. In order to put my findings in context, however, it is necessary to first present the complicated and extensive debate over the theory currently used to describe the behavior of battered women who kill.

THE BATTERED WOMAN

Who is a "battered woman?" Lenore Walker offers this description:

> A battered woman is a woman who is repeatedly subjected to any forceful physical or psychological behavior by a man in order to coerce her to do something he wants her to do without any concern for her rights. Battered women include wives or women in any form of intimate relationships with men. Furthermore, in order to be classified as a battered woman, the couple must go through the battering cycle at least twice. Any woman may find herself in an abusive relationship with a man once. If it occurs a second time, and she remains in that situation, she is defined as a battered woman.[84]

Feminist scholars find Walker's definition problematic for several reasons. "Battered women include wives or women in any form of intimate relationships with men:" Martha Mahoney criticizes Walker's assumption

---

[84] Walker, *The Battered Woman*, xv.

that violence occurs only in heterosexual relationships?[85] Although less information is available regarding partner violence in same-sex relationships, recent studies suggest that abuse occurs as frequently among lesbian and gay as among heterosexual couples.[86] By referring only to a man and woman, or a husband and wife, Walker may prevent many other people from recognizing themselves as living in violence. Feminist activists and academics, Elizabeth Schneider argues, must continue to highlight the "particular experience of woman-abuse, shaped by understandings of male domination in heterosexual relationships, while including in our understanding the ways in which power and control operate in all intimate relationships."[87]

Although Walker includes a psychological element of abuse in her definition, Mahoney notes that she immediately shifts her focus to physical abuse and the cycle of violence in identifying a battering relationship.[88] Walker states that the woman must experience the battering cycle at least twice; Mahoney finds this troublesome. If a woman has only been physically abused once by her partner, isn't that sufficient? Psychologist Angela Browne, who has conducted research with Walker, acknowledges that often the severity of abuse cannot be measured by the number of attacks: "Though women who are assaulted 'only once' are rarely labeled as battered and still less often studied, any use of violence in a relationship can dramatically alter the balance of power, destroying a sense of openness and trust on the part of the woman and resulting in a permanent sense of inequality, threat, and loss."[89]

Walker's definition may also risk doing exactly what she counsels others not to do: place the blame on the woman. Walker states that any woman may find herself in an abusive relationship, but only one who

---

[85] Martha Mahoney, "Legal Images of Battered Women," *Michigan Law Review* 90.1 (October 1991): 9. In Massachusetts, Debra Reid killed her lesbian partner and was sentenced to 9 to 14 years in prison. Ms. Reid was one of four members of the Framingham Eight who declined to be interviewed for this project.

[86] Angela Browne, "Violence against Women by Male Partners: Prevalence, Outcomes, and Policy Implications," *American Psychologist* 48.10 (October 1993): 1078. See also Claire Renzetti, "Building a Second Closet: Third Party Responses to Victims of Lesbian Partner Abuse," in *Understanding Partner Violence: Prevalence, Causes, Consequences & Solutions,* ed. Sandra M. Stith and Murray A. Straus (Minneapolis: National Council on Family Relations, 1995), 58-66, which cites studies finding that 25 percent of lesbians have been physically abused by their female partners, and that 47 percent of a lesbian and gay male sample had used physical aggression in their relationships.

[87] Elizabeth M. Schneider, "Particularity and Generality," *New York University Law Review* 67 (June 1992): 547-8. Reprinted with permission.

[88] Mahoney, 28.

[89] Browne, *When Battered Women Kill*, 14.

remains in it after the second battering incident may be classified as a battered woman. This focus on the reaction of the woman to the violence, Mahoney contends, contains the dangerous implication that she has assumed the label "battered woman" through her own behavior.[90]

Walker and other domestic violence theorists have increasingly emphasized incidents of physical violence in their characterizations of battered women.[91] Although precise definitions highlighting assault may be useful in describing battered women before the law, some scholars argue that they may also be problematic. A description too focused on physical striking may allow many abused women to distance themselves from this category, denying its relevance to their own experiences. Even a single violent act is usually accompanied by more pervasive psychological abuse and control; women often state that it is the psychological abuse that is so debilitating.[92] Martha Mahoney therefore expands Walker's definition. She describes a battered woman as a "woman who experiences the violence against her as determining her thoughts, emotions, or actions, including her efforts to cope with the violence itself."[93] Battering, according to Mahoney, is a form of coercion; stressing the controlling aspects of an abusive relationship creates a clearer link between domestic violence and the historical oppression of women in a male-dominated society. In addition, describing the violence in this manner may help more women recognize and understand their situations as being abusive. "Women may find the current terminology of battering stigmatizing or alienating, yet be willing to admit that they have experienced inappropriate control attempts by their partners, including assaults on their capacity to separate from 'bad' marriages,"[94] Mahoney argues.

Although scholars argue that a definition highlighting control and power would be more accurate for lives of women, they also acknowledge that a more inclusive and nebulous description could create new problems for battered women in legal and legislative areas. Schneider explains that an

---

[90] Mahoney, 28.

[91] Angela Browne's definition of battered women also stresses incidents of violence: "[B]attered women are those who have been struck repeatedly, often experiencing several different kinds of physically violent actions in one incident, and usually, by the time they are identified, having experience a series of such incidents, each consisting of a cluster of violent acts." Browne, *When Battered Women Kill*, 13.

[92] In a study of 234 physically abused women, 229 (98 percent) reported experiencing emotional abuse in their relationships as well. One hundred fifty-nine (72 percent) of the women stated that the emotional abuse had more impact than the physical abuse. Diane Follingstad et al., "The Role of Emotional Abuse in Physically Abusive Relationships," *Journal of Family Violence* 5.2 (1990): 113.

[93] Mahoney, 93. Reprinted with permission.

[94] Ibid., 69.

effort to expand the definition of battering "must confront the complexity and messiness that are characteristic of all intimate relationships. The particularity that makes battering legally cognizable thus limits the generality that reflects a more accurate vision of battering relationships."[95] By placing domestic violence on a continuum of control within relationships, theorists risk negating the special nature of battered women's cases.

Linked to this definitional debate is a struggle over whether the term "battered woman" is an apt or acceptable label. Terminology is extremely important, for both society's and the individual woman's understanding of her situation. Both Mahoney and Schneider argue that phrases such as "battered woman" or "abused woman" focus on the woman, rather than on the batterer, and in so doing, encourage people to view the woman as the problem in the relationship.[96] In addition, these terms may depict the woman and her characteristics in a manner that, as Schneider explains, "fails to communicate the range and complexity of her experiences. This term makes her, not the experiences she has suffered, the problem."[97] Yet there are those theorists who choose to endorse a more focused term such as "battered woman" over "spouse abuse" which is not gender-specific and implies that men are abused in these relationships as often as women.[98] Words such as "domestic" or "family," they argue, also tend to suggest that the abuse is less severe or significant than other forms of violence.

As a possible solution to these terminological pitfalls, some feminist theorists have encouraged using the phrase: "a woman who has (or had) a relationship with a battering man." This alternative terminology, Schneider argues, "describes the woman as a survivor of a relationship with a controlling man, rather than defining the totality of a woman by the behavior of the man with whom she has a relationship."[99] Employing this description, the woman no longer becomes completely defined by her experience with her abuser. In addition, by moving away from the label "battered woman" and its associated helpless and dysfunctional stereotypes, a woman may be less ashamed to describe herself and her experiences in this way.

---

[95] Schneider, "Particularity and Generality," 539.
[96] Mahoney, 25. For further discussion of the terminology associated with violence against women, see Schneider, "Particularity and Generality," 530; Browne, *When Battered Women Kill*, 13; and Mahoney, 25.
[97] Schneider, "Particularity and Generality," 530.
[98] Almost one million incidents of partner violence occur each year, and about 85 percent of the victims are women. Department of Justice, *Violence Between Intimates*. Source: National Crime Victimization Survey, 1992-6.
[99] Schneider, "Particularity and Generality," 531.

THE BATTERED WOMAN SYNDROME

The law of self-defense, as previously explained, rests on the premise that a person may use reasonable force against another person when she believes herself to be in imminent danger and the use of that force is necessary to avoid unlawful bodily harm.[100] What is essential here is the *reasonableness* of the defendant's perception. It is this fundamental element that battered women have difficulty meeting before the eyes of a jury.

On the witness stand or in a clemency proceeding, an expert on the battered woman syndrome will testify as to why a woman might not have tried to leave an abusive relationship, and why a battered woman might have reasonably (and justifiably) acted in self-defense at the time of the homicide.[101] Why a battered woman did not leave is usually the first question from the jury, but more important in self-defense cases is the reasonableness of the woman's perception of danger at the moment of the homicide. The purpose of expert testimony on the battered woman syndrome, within both a trial and a commutation proceeding, is primarily to dispel common misconceptions about domestic violence that may bias society against battered women in general. It is important to note that the battered woman syndrome is not intended to be a defense in itself, but a theory used to expand the traditional doctrine of self-defense to accommodate the situations of battered women who have killed their abusers. The battered woman syndrome consists of two processes Walker has identified within abusive relationships: the cycle of violence and learned helplessness.

THE CYCLE OF VIOLENCE

Lenore Walker argues that battering relationships are characterized by a three-phase cycle of violence. The first stage consists of relatively minor incidents of abuse; it is called the tension-building phase.[102] During this period, the woman is hit or verbally degraded, and she attempts to calm her batterer in order to avoid an escalation of violence. "More than anything," Walker explains, "she wants to prevent the batterer's violence from growing. This desire, however, proves to be a sort of double-edged sword,

---

[100] LaFave and Scott, 649.
[101] See Elizabeth Schneider, "Describing and Changing: Women's Self-Defense Work and the Problem of Expert Testimony on Battering," in *Representing...Battered Women Who Kill*, ed. Sara Lee Johann and Frank Osanka (Springfield: Charles C. Thomas, 1989), 78.
[102] Walker, *The Battered Woman*, 56-9. See also Walker, *Terrifying Love*, 42-3.

because her placatory, docile behavior legitimizes his belief that he has the right to abuse her in the first place."[103] The woman tries to make the environment as stress-free as possible, in an attempt to control her batterer's anger and violence. Because the batterer is usually jealous of her friends and family members, the woman may become increasingly isolated as she tries to keep her abuser happy. However, the batterer's actions almost never change in these situations; the woman's attempts to prevent the violence usually prove futile.

As her batterer's reactions become increasingly unpredictable and her attempts at appeasement less effective, the woman eventually withdraws emotionally, sparking increased anger and abuse. "At some point, and often not predictably," Walker explains, "the violence spirals out of control, and an acute battering incident occurs."[104]

The second phase of the cycle is considerably more violent, characterized by increasingly frequent and severe beatings. Walker notes that this phase is "briefer than the first and the third phases. Usually it lasts from two to twenty-four hours, although some women have reported a steady reign of terror for a week or more."[105] Both the batterer and the battered woman sense that the violence is out of control; usually, the woman realizes that she cannot reason with her batterer, and her focus shifts to surviving the attacks. "She does not feel the pain," Walker says, "as much as she feels psychologically trapped and unable to flee the situation. This feeling is usually accompanied by a firm belief that if she does anything to try to resist, her attacker will only become more violent."[106] Phase two encompasses the most acute battering and the woman's worst physical abuse. But, Walker explains, when "there has been physical violence, the battered woman will often minimize her injuries."[107] If at all possible, Walker argues, most women resist seeking help from police or medical professionals after an assault:

> The police are usually called during phase two – if they are called at all. Of the women interviewed, only 10 percent had ever called the police. Many of them stated that they do not call the police because they do not feel the police can deal effectively with the batterers. Statistics confirm this assumption. In Kansas City in 1976, a study found that over

---

[103] Walker, *Terrifying Love*, 43.
[104] Ibid.
[105] Walker, *The Battered Woman*, 60.
[106] Ibid., 62.
[107] Ibid., 63.

80 percent of all women murdered by their men had called for help one to five times prior to being killed.[108]

There is no way for the woman to predict the end of this stage of the battering cycle. "Only the batterers can end the second phase," Walker explains. "The woman's only option is to find a safe place to hide."[109] Once the battering has stopped, the cycle is completed by a loving or contrite phase, when the batterer expresses remorse for his actions and gives the woman reason to believe his behavior will change. During this time, the battered woman may be convinced that the abuse will cease. She is naturally inclined to believe this: her batterer's promises bolster her faith. It is during this stage of the cycle, Walker argues, that the woman experiences the most severe psychological damage. "Now the illusion of absolute interdependency is firmly solidified in the woman's psyche, for in this phase battered women and their batterers really are emotionally dependent on one another – she for his caring behavior, he for her forgiveness."[110] But despite this display of remorse, the battering does not end. Walker's studies show that the cycle of violence will begin again, with the abuse escalating in frequency and severity.

Scholars agree that the cycle of violence has been effectively used by forensic psychologists to explain why a battered woman might act in self-defense. Battered women who kill their abusers usually see the incident provoking the homicide as more severe than prior assaults. This aspect of the battered woman syndrome relates directly to the imminency requirement of self-defense; the cycle of violence theory describes the unique understanding a woman gains in this situation, a perspective that may not be clear to another observer. Walker argues that battered women become attuned to the patterns of violence and learn to adapt to the behavior of their abusers. As Elizabeth Schneider explains, "subtle motions or threats that may not signal danger to an outsider or to the trier of act acquire added meaning for a battered woman whose survival depends on an intimate knowledge of her assailant."[111] The cycle of violence describes a situation in which a woman becomes so cognizant of danger signals from her batterer that she is able to perceive a change in the level of abuse foretelling her imminent death.

Psychologists testifying on the battered woman syndrome do cite the cycle of violence when discussing a battering relationship. But attorneys,

---

[108] Ibid., 64.
[109] Ibid., 61.
[110] Walker, *Terrifying Love*, 45. For further discussion of the cycle of violence theory, see Walker *Terrifying Love*, 44-5; Walker, *The Battered Woman Syndrome*, 95-104; and Walker, *The Battered Woman*, 55-70.
[111] Schneider, "Equal Rights," 634.

judges, and lawmakers most frequently seize upon the concept of "learned helplessness" to describe the battered woman. Legal scholars argue that this theory may be harmful – even when resulting in the acquittal or release of a woman – because it may fail to account for the reasonableness of her actions. I suggest that it may also present an inaccurate picture of what a woman experiences in a battering relationship.

LEARNED HELPLESSNESS

The result of the cycle of violence and the woman's lack of control over her treatment is what Walker describes as "learned helplessness," an element that is central to the battered woman syndrome: "I interpret [battered women's] behavior as a basic coping mechanism, much like Seligman's (1975) dogs, who used passivity to stay alive. The analogy is the failure for both the dogs and the battered women to develop adequate escape skills."[112]

Martin Seligman, a psychologist at the University of Pennsylvania, performed experiments with dogs in which he placed them in cages and administered electric shocks to them at random moments. Once the dogs learned that the shocks were unpredictable and out of their control, they no longer attempted to escape. Their "learned helplessness response" could only be undone if the dogs were then repeatedly brought to the cage door; they needed to be physically led to safety before they could learn to escape on their own.[113]

Seligman found that, when his research was extended to humans, an individual's *perceptions* of his or her ability to escape were more important than the actual potential for escape. As Walker explains: "Thus, when people are involved, the truth or facts of a situation turn out to be less important than the individual's set of beliefs or perceptions concerning the situation."[114] Walker believes that Seligman's findings may be applied to the cognitive processes and behavior that battered women demonstrate:

> Thus, in applying the learned helplessness concept to battered women, the process of how the battered woman becomes victimized grows clearer. Repeated batterings, like electrical shocks, diminish the woman's motivation to

---

[112] Walker, *The Battered Woman Syndrome*, 3. Reprinted with permission.
[113] For a detailed discussion of the concept of learned helplessness, see Walker, *Terrifying Love*, 49-53; Walker, *The Battered Woman Syndrome*, 86-94; and Walker, *The Battered Woman*, 42-54.
[114] Walker, *Terrifying Love*, 50.

respond. She becomes passive. Secondly, her cognitive ability to perceive success is changed. She does not believe her response will result in a favorable outcome, whether or not it might. Next, having generalized her helplessness, the battered woman does not believe anything she does will alter any outcome, not just the specific situation that has occurred. She says, "No matter what I do, I have no influence." She cannot think of alternatives. She says, "I am incapable and too stupid to learn how to change things." Finally, her sense of emotional well-being becomes precarious. She is more prone to depression and anxiety.[115]

Repeatedly subjected to experiences over which he or she has no control, an individual's motivation to control future outcomes will decrease. In the case of battered women, according to Walker, survival and coping skills are developed at the expense of escape skills. Learned helplessness provides one explanation for why battered women might not leave their abusive partners; Walker paints a picture of women who, like Seligman's dogs, are unable to escape the seemingly random attacks inflicted upon them. "People suffering from learned helplessness are more likely to choose behavioral responses that will have the highest predictability of an effect within the known, or familiar, situation; they avoid responses – like escape, for instance, that launch them into the unknown."[116]

A FLAWED THEORY

Elizabeth Schneider, one of the pioneering attorneys in battered women's self-defense cases,[117] has also been among the most prominent critics of the battered woman syndrome, warning against its potential misuse and misinterpretation:

> Although the term is purely descriptive, its psychological content and the language and import of the term carry a different message. Regardless of its more complex meaning,

---

[115] Walker, *The Battered Woman*, 49-50.
[116] Walker, *Terrifying Love*, 50-1.
[117] Elizabeth Schneider was co-counsel in *State v. Wanrow*, 88 Wash. 2d 221, 559 P. 2d 548 (1977) and co-counsel for *amicus curiae* in *State v. Kelly*, 97 N.J. 178, 487 A. 2d. 364 (1984). She has also worked with the Women's Self-Defense Law Project, founded in 1978 to educate attorneys representing battered women who have defended themselves.

the term "battered women syndrome" has been heard to communicate an explicit but powerful view that battered women are all the same, that they are suffering from a psychological disability and that this disability prevents them from acting "normally."[118]

Schneider argues that the word "syndrome" connotes incapacity; it pathologizes the battered woman and implies that she suffers from a psychological defect. In this sense, the battered woman syndrome sounds remarkably like an impaired mental state defense, a defense that precludes the woman's actions from being judged as reasonable and justified. Although not intended to serve as an insanity or diminished capacity defense, Schneider explains that courts have interpreted battered woman syndrome testimony as a version of an impaired mental state defense for several reasons:

> This is undoubtedly not merely the problem of the term itself – which, again, intends to be simply descriptive – but of the stereotypes that it triggers for lawyers and judges. Courts are more likely to hear and respond to a perception of women as damaged than as reasonable, so presentation of testimony on the battered woman syndrome responds more to and plays on patriarchal attitudes which courts have exhibited toward women and women defendants generally.[119]

Any defense based on mental incapacity will be rejected by the standards of reasonableness. Thus, when presented with a portrait of a woman as psychologically damaged, a jury's evaluation of her behavior may shift to excuse without even considering justification.

Schneider and other theorists believe that the concept of learned helplessness contributes most to the pathologizing, and thus the excusing, of the battered woman and her actions. Although learned helplessness is only one element of the battered woman syndrome, judges, legislators, and laypeople have consistently focused on this theory to describe the battered woman. Learned helplessness emphasizes the victimization of the woman and her lack of control over her life and environment. Women are portrayed as incapable of leaving abusive mates, victims of fear and prolonged violence. The picture of the battered woman resembles a mentally handicapped person; the emphasis is on her inability to act within

---

[118] Schneider, "Describing and Changing," 71-2.
[119] Ibid., 89. See also Browne, *When Battered Women Kill*, 177, and Mahoney, 38-9.

the context of this abuse. In the 1985 case of *State v. Hundley*, the Kansas Supreme Court relied on expert testimony to draw a picture of the battered woman as an emotional and psychological victim:

> The abuse is so severe, for so long a time, and the threat of great bodily harm so constant, it creates a standard mental attitude in its victims. Battered women are terror-stricken people *whose mental state is distorted* and bears a marked resemblance to that of a hostage or a prisoner of war. The horrible beatings they are subjected to brainwash them into believing that there is nothing they can do. They live in constant fear of another eruption of violence. *They become disturbed persons from the torture.* (Italics added)[120]

Schneider argues that portraying women as helpless, passive, and psychologically disturbed is harmful because it reinforces traditional derogatory images of women, but it may be particularly damaging for battered women who have killed because it fails to account for why they eventually acted. Jurors are presented with a description of the battered woman who is helpless and submissive. Any woman who deviates from this model, who seeks help or defends her own life may be seen as abnormal or unreasonable. Experts on the battered woman syndrome often stress, or are *heard* as stressing the woman's helplessness to leave, rather than the circumstances which might make her action of self-defense necessary and reasonable. In focusing on the history of the woman's inaction, Schneider argues, the battered woman syndrome risks portraying any action on her part as contradicting the passive battered woman stereotype. Indeed, courts have judged some battered women as not fitting the helpless model. In the case of *Fennell v. Goolsby*, for example, expert testimony was not admitted because the woman had forced her husband out of the home with an order of protection, and they had been separated for six months when she killed him.[121] Thus, the battered woman syndrome may restrict rather than expand the rights of battered women before the law. Judges may not admit expert testimony, Schneider argues, "in those cases where the woman's actions significantly depart from both the traditional 'male' model of self-defense and the passive 'battered woman' model. If they do

---

[120] *State v. Hundley*, 236 Kan. 461, 693 P. 2d 475 (1985). In the 1984 case of *State v. Kelly*, the expert's testimony described "the feelings of self-blame, isolation, and, above all, fear that plagues these women and leaves them prey to a psychological paralysis that hinders their ability to break free or seek help." *State v. Kelly*, 97 N.J., 195-7, 478 A2d, 372-3.

[121] *Fennell v. Goolsby* 630 F. Supp. 451 (E.D. Pa. 1985). For further discussion of this case, see *Representing . . . Battered Women Who Kill*, ed. Sara Lee Johann and Frank Osanka, 303-5.

admit the testimony they may see its relevance in terms that, even unwittingly, conform to or reinforce those stereotypes."[122] In order to use the battered woman syndrome in her defense, a woman must portray herself as passive and helpless. If her behavior deviates from this passive model, her defense may be challenged. Ironically, the very theory that is intended to justify her behavior may suggest that any self-defensive actions are abnormal and thus unreasonable.

The battered woman syndrome, Schneider contends, threatens to construct a separate category for women, based on their victimization. Expert testimony on the syndrome is based on the description of battered women as a collective group; it is founded upon the premise that women in general, and battered women in particular, share a common experience of sexual discrimination and victimization. Schneider argues that this element of collectivity in the battered woman syndrome highlights a paradox that exists in feminist theory in general. By describing the common characteristics of victims of domestic violence, the battered woman syndrome may actually preclude some women who may not meet the "common" criteria from raising a self-defense claim. Creating a category for descriptive purposes necessarily entails shutting certain people out of that category; the use of the battered woman syndrome and the description of the "average" battered woman may not be flexible enough to accommodate the variety of experiences these women have.[123]

Furthermore, emphasizing women's differences from men, both essential and socially constructed, raises the question of whether difference necessarily implies inferiority.[124] In the case of *State v. Wanrow*, for example, the court referred to the female defendant's "individual physical

---

[122] Schneider, "Describing and Changing," 58.

[123] This description also focuses on the battered woman's character, while studies show that it is the batterer's behavior, not the battered woman's psychological makeup, that predict whether she will act in self-defense. In her study of battered women who killed, Angela Browne found only one predictor linked to the woman: her threats of suicide. "In a test of which variables most clearly distinguished women who had killed their abusive mates from women who were abused but took no lethal action, seven key dynamics were identified: the frequency with which abusive incidents occurred; the severity of the women's injuries; the frequency of forced or threatened sexual acts by the man; the man's drug use; the frequency of his intoxication; the man's threats to kill; and the woman's threats to commit suicide." Browne, *When Battered Women Kill*, 127.

[124] As legal scholar Martha Minow explains: "Although some people have resisted and challenged the meanings assigned to them, recipients of labels are often unable to control the many layers of negative association those labels carry. The web of negative associations assigned to the outsider complicates any effort to resist the denigration implied by difference." Martha Minow, "Justice Engendered," *Harvard Law Review* (November 1987): 37-8.

handicaps which are a product of our nation's sex discrimination." (Italics added)[125] Schneider argues that by stressing women's differences from men, in terms of the reasonableness of their perceptions on issues such as equal force, imminency, and retreat, the battered woman syndrome may merely restate traditional views of female inferiority. As legal theorist Kimberly Fraser explains: "The possibility of reinforcing gender stereotypes remains because the reasonable woman standard also highlights the differences between men and women, and unless the 'differentness' of the female perspective is valued then the progress of truly just woman self-defense claims will continue to be inhibited."[126] Again, the woman's actions may be viewed through the lens of excuse before they are even considered within the realm of justification.

Angela Browne argues that "the issue is not the development of a new standard of self-defense for women, but the adjustment of existing statues to account for differences in the experiences of men and women – particularly women faced with a male assailant, and women who are the victims of repeated assaults by one assailant – so that the same standard can be applied to all victims."[127] But the battered woman syndrome does risk creating a new and distinct standard of self-defense, based on "the reasonable woman" or "the reasonable battered woman" category. Mahoney and Schneider contend that the problem lies in the syndrome's vulnerability to "distortion in culture and law."[128] I suggest that it derives from the notion of learned helplessness itself. We must go beyond merely challenging the interpretation of the theory: we must reexamine its actual content. The criminal justice system may determine battered women's acts as reasonable within the framework of self-defense – if it considers social, rather than psychological theories to describe their behavior.

ALTERNATIVES TO LEARNED HELPLESSNESS

Some scholars argue that battered women are not the helpless victims the battered woman syndrome often seems to describe. Instead, they are survivors who, like other reasonable people, attempt to save their lives when faced with danger. Sociologist Edward Gondolf and social worker Ellen Fisher propose that the helplessness might actually exist within the society around them that fails to offer another route of escape, while

---

[125] *State v. Wanrow*, 88 Wash. 2d 240, 559 P. 2d 559.
[126] Kimberly Fraser, *Defending the Battered Woman Who Kills*, Paper Submitted for LLM Degree, Harvard University, 1991, 69.
[127] Browne, *When Battered Women Kill*, 175.
[128] Mahoney, 42.

Martha Mahoney stresses the danger of separation assault as a real obstacle to battered women's freedom from violence.

Gondolf and Fisher, authors of *Battered Women as Survivors: An Alternative to Treating Learned Helplessness*, challenge the concept of learned helplessness as it has traditionally been applied to battered women. They argue that the battered woman syndrome's inherent flaws are indicated by the fundamental question it originally set out to answer: The question "Why don't women leave?" is problematic because it implicitly blames the woman for the situation, rather than looking at the role that the man should play in stopping the abuse. The question should be reformulated to ask "Why do men batter?" Or "Why does society tolerate men who batter?" As Gondolf and Fisher explain, when a man assaults a person outside the home, we challenge his behavior. "The assumption is that there is something wrong with him, not the victim, that has to be addressed. But when a man assaults his wife or partner, the tendency is to focus first on why the victim doesn't have sense enough to avoid the violence."[129]

Gondolf and Fisher argue that learned helplessness is an inaccurate description of a battered woman's response to her situation. They base their alternative survivor theory on several empirical studies, including those of Lenore Walker. These studies support the hypothesis that battered women are not helpless victims resigned to a life of abuse, but instead are active survivors thwarted in their attempts to leave by real legal and social obstacles.

Gondolf and Fisher quote this finding within Lenore Walker's study of battered women:

> *As the violence escalated, so did the probability that the battered women would seek help.* While only 14 percent sought help after the first battering incident, 22 percent did after the second, 31 percent after one of the worst, and 49 percent sought help after the last incident. About one-quarter of the women left temporarily immediately after each battering incident, although these were not necessarily the same women each time. (Italics added)[130]

---

[129] Gondolf and Fisher, 19.
[130] Walker, *The Battered Woman Syndrome*, 27, as quoted in Gondolf and Fisher, 18. According to a 1996 national study, approximately 77 percent of female victims of nonlethal intimate violence actively defended themselves. About 60 percent used nonconfrontational means, such as trying to escape or calling the police, and about 17 percent confronted the abuser by struggling, shouting, or chasing him. Only two percent of the latter group defended themselves with a weapon. Department of Justice, Bureau of Justice Statistics, *Violence by Intimates: Analysis of Data on Crimes by Current or*

The question "Why don't women leave?" is inappropriate, Gondolf and Fisher argue, because it assumes women don't leave. Many battered women *do* leave. Battered women also frequently call the police for help or seek restraining orders against their abusers in court.[131] The criminal justice system is slow to act on these cases, or ignores them altogether. Furthermore, a battered woman often learns that a piece of paper will not actually prevent further abuse at the hands of the batterer; it may even provoke his increased anger and her own death.[132] Walker herself cited a statistic in *The Battered Woman*, mentioned previously: "In Kansas City in 1976, a study found that over 80 percent of all women murdered by their men had called for help one to five times prior to being killed."[133]

The police are not alone in ignoring women's calls for help. Gondolf and Fisher note that other community service providers also fail to assist battered women:

> If learned helplessness is a valid conception, it is ironically prevalent in the system of helping sources... Granted, the battered woman's contact with the clergy, human services, police, and legal assistance may at times be tentative. But the women meet an equally tentative response from the helpers. Malpractice suits, no-risk clauses, privatization of services, severe funding cutbacks, and a laissez-faire public attitude have brought reluctance rather than initiative to the helping professions.[134]

If a woman chooses to leave, she finds a range of societal obstacles in her way. It is extremely hard for a woman to leave her marriage and family when people continue to view this action, regardless of the reasons behind it, as failure and abandonment on her part. She may also lack financial

---

Former Spouses, Boyfriends, and Girlfriends (Washington, D.C., March 1998, NCJ 167237). In an earlier study of 109 battered women, 88 percent said they did leave at some point after being assaulted. Dobash and Dobash, 144.

[131] According to recent national statistics, in 1996, 56 percent of female victims of intimate violence called the police. Department of Justice, *Violence by Intimates*. In her study of police response to domestic violence, Lee Bowker found that 53 percent of the battered women in the sample had called the police at least once, and 12 percent had used them on six or more occasions. Lee H. Bowker, "Battered Wives and the Police: A National Study of Usage and Effectiveness," *Police Studies* 7.2 (Summer 1984): 86.

[132] Many women are killed after seeking help through the police or the courts. In March of 1992, Shirley Lowry, a grandmother, was stabbed 19 times by her boyfriend in the courthouse where she had gone to seek an order of protection. Nancy Gibbs, "Till Death Do Us Part," *Time*, 18 January 1993, 38-45.

[133] Walker, *The Battered Woman*, 64.

[134] Gondolf and Fisher, 22-3.

resources: a battered woman frequently has only an allowance for household expenses and the clothes she wears.[135] Furthermore, she may have nowhere to go: there are few shelters available for women who move out of their homes. In the state of Massachusetts, less than 30 percent of battered women are able to find protection in shelters.[136] The majority of women are turned away for lack of adequate space, or because there are no facilities for families. If a woman does have children, she might justifiably fear leaving them with a man who has already threatened or harmed her, and possibly them as well.[137]

Thus, community passivity and economic barriers are largely responsible for a woman's inability to escape her violent partner. Gondolf and Fisher call for better coordination, greater activism, and a more serious approach by police, mental health providers, shelters, and legal services to help abused women find safety.

Martha Mahoney, on the other hand, focuses on the batterer's behavior to explain why a woman might not successfully leave the relationship. "*Separation assault*," she explains, "is the attack on the woman's body and volition in which her partner seeks to prevent her from leaving, retaliate for the separation, or force her to return."[138] Mahoney stresses that the batterer poses the greatest threat to the woman's safe escape; separation usually does not end the violence. Statistics from the United States government reveal that in almost 75 percent of all domestic assaults, the woman was divorced or separated from her batterer at the time of the incident.[139] The constant danger a woman faces must be viewed within this context of the batterer's efforts to control her and challenge her autonomy.[140] In addition, the concept of separation assault

---

[135] Gillespie, 150.

[136] In Massachusetts, for every two women sheltered, five are turned away. Nationwide, it is estimated that more than one-half of homeless women are on the street because they are fleeing domestic violence. Senate Judiciary Committee, *Women and Violence: Hearings before the U.S. Senate Judiciary Committee*, Senate Hearing 101-939, pt. 2, 29 August 1990 and 11 December 1990, 128; 79.

[137] Thyfault, 32-3. In families experiencing wife abuse, children are physically abused at a rate of 1,500 times higher than the national average. In addition, the most serious cases of child abuse entering emergency rooms are extensions of battering against the mother; 70 percent of the serious and 80 percent of the fatal injuries to these children are inflicted by abusive men. Senate Judiciary Committee, *Women and Violence*, 142.

[138] Mahoney, 65.

[139] Department of Justice, Bureau of Justice Statistics, *Report to the Nation*, 2nd ed. (Washington, D.C., March 1988), 3.

[140] The most common motivation husbands give for killing their wives is a feeling of abandonment or fear that they were losing control over these women. Noel Cazenave and Margaret Zahn, "Women, Murder, and Male Domination: Police Reports of Domestic

takes a significant step towards focusing on the batterer, not the battered woman. Mahoney argues, "Exposing control attempts reveals the woman's struggle, rather than defining her according to the behavior of her assailant."[141]

However, it is important to note that Mahoney offers the theory of separation assault as an addition to, rather than a substitute for Walker's theory: "I do not mean to criticize... the psychological theory underlying the battered woman syndrome, or even the particular theory of learned helplessness,"[142] Mahoney writes. I argue, however, that the notion of learned helplessness should be abandoned in favor of these other theories to explain the behavior of battered women who kill in self-defense. The concepts of separation assault and society's indifference to her abuse can explain a battered woman's perceptions of danger as reasonable by encouraging examination of the real external forces, rather than psychological deficiencies, that may prevent her escape.

In light of the debate and conflicting theories concerning the battered woman syndrome, I have attempted to answer several questions in my research with battered women convicted of killing their abusers. First, I hope to understand how these women actually view *themselves*. How do they feel about the label "battered woman?" Do they present themselves as helpless victims, active survivors, or somewhere in between? Have these descriptions changed over time? How accurate is the battered woman syndrome, the cycle of violence, and learned helplessness, in relation to their lives and experiences? Is a theory of society's indifference or separation assault a better lens through which to view their behavior? Finally, why did these women eventually act, and how do they themselves account for their action? Do they take responsibility for it, do they excuse it, do they feel as though they need to be forgiven? Is commutation an adequate solution for their cases, or do they believe they should be pardoned, based on a wrongful conviction? What should the criminal justice system consider in judging these cases, and can this lead to a new understanding of what battered women's acts should mean for society? The following chapter attempts to address these questions by listening to the women themselves.

Homicide in Chicago and Philadelphia" (paper presented at the annual meeting of the American Society of Criminology, Atlanta, Georgia, October 1986).
[141] Mahoney, 69.
[142] Ibid., 42.

CHAPTER FOUR

SELF-REPRESENTATIONS OF BATTERED WOMEN WHO KILLED

> "I didn't know that there was a name for what was happening to me. I knew that it was wrong, and I knew that I didn't like it, and I knew that it had to stop, but I didn't know that there were other women like me. I didn't learn all of this until I came to jail."
>
> –Patricia Hennessy

A central question emerges: To what extent does the battered woman syndrome accurately describe women who kill their abusers? Although their formal appeals for clemency cite the battered woman syndrome, this theory contains elements that seem at odds with the women's self-perceptions, as well as with their claims of self-defense. To flush out these apparent inconsistencies, I wanted these four women to have the opportunity to confront the labels placed on their lives and actions by others. Do their experiences suggest that the battered woman syndrome needs to be reformulated? How does the battered woman syndrome influence the amount of culpability they feel for their actions? Do they believe they should be excused as victims, or judged as justified actors? Finally, do the women feel that commutations or pardons would be just outcomes of their cases?

In this chapter, I discuss the battered woman syndrome as a category for redefining for these women's life stories. The theory has constructed a community for the women, legitimizing their past victimization and providing them with a new label: survivors. Next, I explore the applicability of each element of the battered woman syndrome to these women's lives. Although the cycle of violence, for example, appears to adequately describe their experiences, the concept of learned helplessness is challenged by these women's stories of leaving and seeking help. I will argue that the obstacles to their escape may be found in the real risk of separation assault and society's indifference to their abuse rather than in the women's inaccurate perceptions of alternatives to violence. The final section of the chapter investigates the women's beliefs regarding their moral culpability and the legal standards to which they should be held. It describes the complexities of their clemency appeals and the definitions of justice for battered women who kill.

REDEFINITION

Throughout their lives, most of these women never knew that there was a name for what was happening to them; "domestic violence" and "battered woman" were unfamiliar terms with no bearing on their lives. "I'd never seen the term 'battered woman,'" Elaine says. "And I don't know if there was a term, 'battered woman.' I mean, towards the end of my abuse, that was the first time that I heard 'battered woman,' but it didn't click. And I really didn't know about shelters or anything else." Many of the women only heard this description after they had been incarcerated.

The label of "battered woman" first struck some of the women as stigmatizing and limiting. Shannon had difficulty reconciling her own feelings of independence with a weak and passive stereotype. The image of the victim was incompatible with her perception of herself as invincible:

> Cause I didn't want to be labeled like that. That's like, as a drug addict, you don't want to be labeled as a drug addict, but you are, you're in denial, and that was me, I was in denial. Because here I am, an African-American woman, I am a strong woman that can handle anything. I had been up against the worst of things in my life, I mean I can write a novel on my life. From my childhood. And it's like, nothing's supposed to break me, I'm supposed to remain strong, hold my head up high, and be proud of who I am, you know, and don't let nothing get in my way.

But despite her initial reaction to the term "battered woman," and its associated images, Shannon, and the other women I spoke with, quickly found a major benefit in claiming this identity. By describing their experiences based on this category, they were able to discover common themes within their life stories. Ironically, it was only in prison that these women were able to find a safe and validating community. Joining others, they gained a new understanding of their past relationships.

In prison, Lisa and other women formed a support group that would later become the organizing force around the Framingham Eight's appeals for clemency: "We started Battered Women Fighting Back, a group for women who were in prison for killing their abusers. We were all in a domestic violence counseling group, but then we found out there were women who had killed their batterers." For these women who had grown accustomed to living in terror within their own homes or neighborhoods, prison offered both the safety and support that society had failed to extend.

As Elaine notes, prison offered the first opportunity for most of these women to speak openly about the violence:

> Getting together was one of the best moments and most memorable experiences of my entire life. I'll never forget it, it was the most empowering. Because we still had a lot of trouble, you couldn't talk about it that much. People still didn't understand, and we were afraid to be put down anymore, like our batterers did to us. So when we got together and we all knew we were in the same boat, we were able to share, we were able to learn about the cycle of violence, and that it wasn't our fault, we didn't deserve it. There we were, sitting in prison, thinking that we deserved every beating we got, that we deserved to die, that we shouldn't even be alive. So, it was a very important part of my life.

This support group the women formed within prison walls provided an education that radically altered their lives and views of the past. Through the process of redefinition, previously accepted events assumed new interpretations. These women no longer viewed the violence they had experienced as normal or deserved: they now defined it as abuse. "Women's understandings of what happened to them change over time," feminist scholar Liz Kelly explains. "Many factors contribute to this, including the creation of terms (such as 'battering' or 'marital' rape) that allow women to name experiences previously silenced, the personal development of the woman over time, and the availability of a supportive and accepting social network."[143] The community these women created was based on a particular collective experience. They were linked by a common bond of victimization. Coming together within prison, the women recognized that they were not alone, that the violence was not their fault, and that there was a name for what they had experienced: the battered woman syndrome.

---

[143] Liz Kelly, "How Women Define Their Experiences of Violence," in *Feminist Perspectives on Wife Abuse,* ed. Kersti Yllo and Michelle Bograd (Newbury Park, CA: Sage Publications, 1988), 128.

VALIDATION OF VICTIMIZATION

On initial questioning, all of the women felt that the battered woman syndrome fit their experiences and aptly described the abuse they had endured. "It was all me, it was all me," Shannon says. "The cycle of violence, the verbal abuse, the emotional abuse, the psychological abuse, it was all me. He would cry, and he would tell me he was sorry, that things would get better, and I always believed that things would get better, I always believed him." In the context of learning about this theory of intimate violence, Patricia discovered remarkable similarities between her experiences and the stories of others:

> When I started learning about the cycle of violence, it was amazing. Oh my God, I thought. It was amazing, amazing that all of us that were in this group, how much alike our stories are, they're alike, but they're different. But it's like my story is every battered woman's story. They're all the same. It's amazing, and even women in here, who didn't defend their lives but were in battering relationships, it's just so on the mark. It's just so right on.

The concept of the battered woman syndrome allowed these women to connect their individual stories to a larger structure, to gain comfort from the shared experiences of others. In the process, this new theory provided legitimacy for their past perceptions and behavior: it validated their victimization. Patricia felt tremendous relief in learning about a theory that confirmed the reasonableness of her reactions. Throughout her relationship, she had believed that she deserved to be beaten and was merely imagining the severity of the abuse:

> I mean, it was like me, me, me. I couldn't believe it. It was kind of a relief, because, I guess, through the battering you feel that maybe it was your fault, that things that you did probably pissed him off, that you didn't have supper on the table, things like that. And then the mind games that they play with you. They really have you thinking that you're crazy, out of your mind. You know, he'd say something and then I'd ask, "Why did you just say that to me?" And he'd say, "Say what? I didn't say anything, what, are you crazy?" And I'd be like, "My God, I'm hallucinating, I'm hearing voices." (laughs) You know, you really doubt your sense of reality. So when they came to me in prison, it was like, I'm not crazy, you know. It was kind of a relief. Even though I was in big trouble, and I still am, it was kind of a relief, knowing that I'm not mental and I'm not crazy, you know what I mean?

Like Patricia, meeting with the support group also led Lisa to look back at her past through a new lens. Learning about domestic violence and the battered woman syndrome enabled her to revise her own life story, to view the abuse and her responses to it differently. Defining herself as a victim involved a revision of past events and their previously accepted meanings:

> At the time, I felt ashamed. I was alone. It's something that every battered woman feels, it's something that's very normal. And you have to make it better, the woman's got to make it better. Towards the end, it got so bad that he never showed remorse anymore. That's why I knew it was coming to a point, I think. Now I know the terms and terminology, and all of that, and I didn't know that before. But I knew that it was in his eyes, and his voice. I know all the terminology now, the reasoning, and why, and I can look at it now as an escalation period that would have never came down.

The concept and terminology of the cycle of violence have provided Lisa with a new context for her past emotions and reactions. In appropriating the language of the battered woman syndrome, all four women have been able to understand their reactions to the abuse as reasonable.

Most of these women also recognized a pattern of victimization in their lives, abuse that they were now learning was unacceptable. Shannon, Lisa, and Elaine had all witnessed or experienced violence in their families or past intimate relationships. They were now redefining a lifetime of abuse as wrong. As Shannon explains, "I've been in abusive relationships. And I always thought that it was O.K., that if people beat on me that meant they loved me, that this was the way that they showed me that they loved me, you know." Lisa also says that she has radically revised her understanding of her past treatment and her role in it:

> As a child, it was something that I grew up with. Brutalized and molested. It was the norm, it was normal. And now I know, and I've learned from it, and I've survived it, and now I can actually talk about it and not be ashamed, because it did happen to me, and it wasn't my fault. I had always thought it was my fault.

VICTIMS, AGAIN?

Collectively, these women have recognized a new phase of victimization within their life stories. They now believe that the criminal justice system is reproducing the control and oppression they experienced within their relationships. Lisa feels that her current incarceration is remarkably similar to her past abuse:

> I had to await trial, and during that awaiting trial, I was locked up 22 hours a day. And it was a prisoner of war camp. I mean, I was prisoner in my first life, and then when I came to prison, I was just treated terribly, under locked up conditions.

Patricia also compares her experience with the criminal justice system to her past abusive relationship. She uses terminology such as "battered," "beaten," and even "defending my life," in describing her current fight for clemency:

> You know what bothers me with this whole legal system, and the commutation thing is really stressing me, it's that it's one thing for me to tell my story to help other people, I've got no problem with that, I'll do what I can if I can prevent other people from being in my place, but what bothers me is, I had to sit in front of these people — not to put them down — and defend my life again. It's like I was begging for my life, and I don't like that feeling. I've fought for my life long and hard, and I felt battered, they dogged me, they dogged me . . . I mean, I was in tears the whole time, I mean, here they sit in judgment, and they've never been slapped a day in their life, they've never been there, they don't have any inclination of what it's like to be beaten. And here they are, drilling me, making me answer to them, making me beg for my life. It was like I was defending my life all over again. I felt so battered when I left there. It was awful, awful. I don't feel that I should have to do that, and now they want us to do that again for the advisory board. Please, you know. They've got the whole thing on tape, you wanna see me cry, press the button.

Shannon also equates her treatment by the law to her batterer's control:

> And it's like, we've already been convicted and tried, and it's like we're going through it all over again. Because this is an oppressive system. You're always told what to do, what not to do, how to do it, when to do it. You cannot move until I tell you to move, you cannot eat until I tell you to eat. You cannot sleep until I tell you to sleep. And when I think about it, it's the same thing that I went

through with José. The same things I went through with José I'm going through in this prison.

Recognizing this double-victimization has become essential to the women's quest for justice – they believe that the legal system's failure to identify them as victims has led them to where they are today. "Now I'm a victim again," Elaine says, "and they've made it into an even larger problem, when it could have probably been solved, if the public, if society, if the system knew how to handle it better from day one." Elaine feels that the judge's refusal to admit her batterer's history of violence prevented her from receiving a fair trial:

> All of my battering wasn't allowed into the trial. They allowed maybe one instance of abuse, and then they tried to discredit it. They wouldn't allow self-defense. The judge said, "I see it sticking its head out there, and I'm not going to allow it. I don't want to hear it. And I don't want to hear about the history of abuse. That has no bearing here. I only want to hear about the incident itself."— That's what he said.

Lisa notes that the courts do acknowledge victimization, but ironically, the term generally refers to the batterer:

> As you go through the process of the court system, they always name him as the victim, and that pisses me off. Because *we* were victims. So yeah, we're labeled victims, but in the right manner, because if you look at society, they always label him as the victim, because he's dead. That's true to a certain extent, but we're the victim too, so we have to deal with that, and that's why the victim label is O.K. I would have been dead, in a short time, Tommy would have killed me. I *know* he would have. I *know* he would have.

This process of redefinition, based on the theory of the battered woman syndrome, has provided the women with a new legal option. Through their clemency appeals, they have been able to tell their revised stories publicly for the first time, renaming their abuse as criminal and themselves as victims. As Elaine explains, "they used to call us murderers, but at least now they call us battered women."

FROM VICTIMS TO SURVIVORS

Their victimized pasts, shared with others, have become a source of empowerment for these women, both legally and personally. Validating their past victimization has in turn led to a recognition of their status as survivors — they have arrived at a new stage within their life stories. "We're not the ones with the problem," Patricia says. "I think the men that are doing the abusing are the ones that should be going to counseling forever in their lives." The victim label now seems incongruous with the women's feelings of strength and the actions they are taking to gain their freedom. Lisa does not see herself as a victim: "Not anymore, I'm not a victim. I'm too strong for that now. I see myself as a survivor. Of a life that I don't think many people would have survived."

These women have come to view themselves as survivors, reinterpreting their past abuse as evidence. This knowledge in turn has enabled them to educate other women beyond the prison community. "I've grown," Shannon says. "I'm very remorseful that it happened, because this is a man that I loved, but in the same process, it's helped me, and it's changed my life, and other people's lives. When I speak, people are hearing what I'm saying to them." Patricia also feels that acknowledging her past victimization has altered her life story and provided her with new strength. "I've learned a lot," she says. "I've learned that I'm not alone. And I've learned that I can help other people, because of what I went through. And I've also learned how strong I am. I'm still alive. I was a victim, *was*." All of these women stress that they do not want sympathy for their pasts; they want understanding and action. "I don't want people to feel sorry for me," Patricia emphasizes, "I just want people to open their eyes, to see what's going on."

The battered woman syndrome has constructed a new supportive community for these women; it has offered a theoretical framework within which they can openly discuss their shared experiences. It has led to their personal and legal empowerment by validating the violence as both wrong and criminal. But a question remains: Have these women entirely accepted the language of the battered woman syndrome? Are their own life stories consistent with this theory?

THE BATTERED WOMAN SYNDROME

THE CYCLE OF VIOLENCE

Through further questioning, it becomes clear that one aspect of the battered woman syndrome is most relevant to these women's experiences. All of them believe that their relationships with their abusers were characterized by a recognizable cycle of violence; the terms they use to describe this cycle reflect Lenore Walker's description of escalating violence within a battering relationship. Elaine, in describing her experiences with Jerry, says that "there was a definite cycle, a honeymoon period, and verbal abuse leading up to violence." Shannon also talks about the remorse that always followed José's most violent episodes: "He threatened me with a gun on Easter Sunday in 1989, the week before he died. He put a gun to my head and threatened to kill me. He said, 'Bitch, I'll kill you before you leave me.' I called my aunt and told her about this. I told her if something happens to me, José did it. Later he said he loved me and started to cry."

In the beginning stages of their relationships, many of the women remained with their abusers out of love. They felt committed to these men, and they had faith that things would improve. "It's like when a kid does something," Patricia explains, "you hate what they're doing, but feelings aren't like a faucet, you can't turn them off and on. It's hard, when that person's acting badly and abusing you, when you love them and want to believe that that nice person's still inside there, and that they're going to stop." Looking back, Shannon also recognizes her batterer's gradual transformation:

> In the beginning of the relationship, everything was fine. But about six months into the relationship, there was the first time: a verbal argument and then a black eye. And then it just progressed and escalated, and I took beatings maybe four or five times a day. With José, the beatings were some of the worst that I had ever took in my life. I could tell stories.

Lisa also describes what Walker refers to as a battered woman's attunement to the violence and her efforts to end the beatings by changing her own behavior: "I used to say, well, it wasn't that bad, I can deal with it, maybe if I didn't do this, or I won't do that next time, or I won't say this, react in this way, you know. And you have to make it better, the woman's got to make it better. It's put upon you, you believe that you're the one that has to make it better."

Yet, despite Lisa's attempts to calm her abuser's anger, she knew the violence was spiraling out of control: "Being beaten, you also have flashbacks of other bad times, and one was worse than the other, so you start thinking of what could happen. And I used to tell Tommy just to kill me, because I just wanted it over with. I just wanted it to end."

All four women believe that their relationships underwent definite cycles of abuse that closely resembled Lenore Walker's theory. This characterization, they feel, is an remarkably accurate description of their batterers' behavior and their fruitless attempts at appeasement.

LEARNED HELPLESSNESS

While all of the women tell stories that support Lenore Walker's concept of the cycle of violence, their accounts are less consistent with her notion of learned helplessness. In fact, the absence of passivity in the women's accounts of both their past and current imprisonment is striking.

"There were times I felt so hopeless," Elaine says about her marriage, "but I wasn't completely dead, I kept trying." All of the women stress their independence. They attempted to create homes for their children, and they maintained jobs and careers while struggling to overcome daily threats to their bodies and minds. A combination of despair and faith existed in all of these women's lives. Shannon rooted her independent self-image in women's traditional role within her culture:

> I've always been a real independent person, doing things for myself, and I never wanted to be a burden to my family members or nothing like that. The background I come from, being from West Indian descent, the women are taught to be strong and to pull together. Nothing can break us, nothing can break us.

These women all describe an almost daily fight to survive, often suffering from severe physical injuries. After one particularly violent beating, Elaine lost consciousness and was taken to a hospital, where she remained in a coma for two months. According to Elaine, the hospital allowed her batterer to make life support decisions for her while on a restraining order for causing her injuries. In the end, the hospital released Elaine to her abuser. Yet the story she tells is not the description of a mentally handicapped, helpless person; this is not a woman who has accepted her fate at the hands of an abusive partner:

> It took me about six months practicing to walk. I could walk, but I could make it to the bathroom and then I'd be exhausted from doing that. So I kept trying to walk a little more each day. I was on the second floor, I remember, and the hallway was inside the apartment, so I'd go all the way down the stairs and I'd fall asleep at the bottom of the stairs because I couldn't make it back up. But I remember, in the coma, I could hear, and I was supposed to have brain damage from being in a coma so long, and being on a machine so long. And I was damned if I was going to be a vegetable. So I used to go down those stairs every day, and even if I couldn't make it up, I'd sleep for an hour, then I'd go back up and go to sleep. And every day I did that until I could make it down without going to sleep, and I made it to the store, and then it seemed when I was mobile again, it started. I mean, there was mental abuse there, like, "Why don't you just die," and, "I have insurance on you."

None of the women invoke the theory of learned helplessness to explain their reactions to the abuse. Asked if they had been helpless at any point during their relationships, they distinguish between feelings of helplessness and hopelessness. They felt hopeless at times, they explain, because their efforts to receive assistance were blocked by others. But, throughout all of their stories, there is no indication that they had resigned themselves to the abuse or had abandoned hope of escape. Despite her fear of her batterer, Patricia never stopped fighting:

> Well, the thing is that I can't ever shut my mouth. You know, if you just shut your mouth, he wouldn't do this. But I'm not like that, I'm sorry. If I'm down on the ground and someone's got a knife up to my throat, I'm going to be screaming, I'm not going out any other way. (laughs) There's this poster that I seen when I was younger, and it's got this mouse, and he's on the ground, and there's this big eagle swooping down, and you know he's going to die, the eagle's got him, and he's got his little finger up, the little mouse, and under it, it says: "ultimate defiance." And it's like, I don't care what you're going to do to me, but I'm going to have my say. I guess I'm like that. Yeah, I said stuff, mostly during the beatings I'd say stuff too. I don't know why I'd do it, I just believe that I should be able to say whatever I want to say. And I shouldn't get beaten for it, you know what I mean? I have my opinion and you're going to hear it. I'll leave a letter, and if you kill me, someone's going to hear it!

At some point during their relationships, each of the women realized that what was going on was wrong, and they refused to passively accept the violence. These women believed they had a right to do more than simply survive the abuse — they believed they had a right to escape it.

WHY DIDN'T THEY LEAVE?

In Chapter Three, I noted that the question "Why didn't they just leave?" is based on several problematic assumptions. First, it places the responsibility for ending the violence on the women, rather than on the batterers. In addition, the question is founded on the false notion that women do not leave; all of the women I spoke with describe numerous attempts to separate from their abusers. Finally, the question implies that leaving is easy, and that it will end the violence. However, these stories show that women must transcend two levels of resistance in order to successfully escape. First, they must overcome their batterers' violent reprisals at their efforts to separate. Then, they must find support from the outside community. Both requirements proved to be tremendous obstacles for all of these women. "People always ask why women don't leave," Lisa says. "People don't get it. I did leave, moved three times. I had gotten restraining orders, changed my windows, my doors, my locks, everything." Shannon, too, repeatedly left her abuser. "But it didn't matter," she says, "because he always found out where I was." With threats and bribery, José would track her down.

SEPARATION ASSAULT

Battered women often speak of the knowledge, through experience, that their abusers will pursue them if they leave. As Shannon explains:

> I was afraid to leave, and I was afraid to stay. You know, if I stayed, I was going to get beaten, if I left, I was going to get beaten. And here I am, caught up in between. And which one is it going to be? It doesn't really matter, because it's going to happen anyway. And wherever I run to, the person I run to, they're going to suffer too. José would break out people's windows, pistol-whip people. Through my relationship with him, the people that knew me, they were being affected by it too, because he didn't care.

The threat these women perceive is real. As noted in the previous chapter's discussion of separation assault, the most dangerous time for a battered woman is when she tries to leave. When battered women are killed, they are more likely than not to be separated from their abusers at the time of death. These four women's stories reflect this, for the violence did increase when they attempted to escape. Either their batterers would immediately locate and punish them, or a lack of adequate resources and shelter would force them to return to a new degree of assault.

SOCIETY'S INDIFFERENCE

The question, "Why didn't you just leave?" meets the same response from each of these women. They all did leave, or attempted to leave, their batterers. Although their accounts differ in detail, the common substance of their stories leads to the next logical question: Why were their attempts ultimately unsuccessful? In addition to separation assault from their batterers, the answer can be found in society's reaction to these women's calls for help. Their batterers' control and society's apathy colluded to create effective barriers to their freedom.

Walker's theory of learned helplessness suggests that the obstacles lie in the battered woman's inaccurate perception of the potential for escape, not in the reality of her situation: "Once the women are operating from a belief of helplessness," Walker writes, "the perceptions become the reality and they become passive, submissive, 'helpless.' They allow things that appear to them to be out of control to actually get out of control."[144] Yet, in focusing on the woman's psychological condition, and by emphasizing the concept of learned helplessness in their descriptions of battered women, psychologists, attorneys, and judges may be ignoring a crucial component in domestic violence: the cages that prevent battered women from escaping. For, even in Seligman's experiments, the bars of the cage played a role in maintaining the dog's captivity; I argue that it essential to recognize the barriers that society has constructed to maintain the battered woman's imprisonment.

The stories of these individual women highlight the reality of these societal barriers. Patricia describes going into hiding with her son:

> We went and stayed in Boston, with a friend, and Timmy had to sleep on this ratty-assed couch, and he had none of his toys, he had nothing, nothing. I don't care if I have nothing, but my kid's not going to live like that. I was there a week, it was Easter, and I couldn't be with my family, and I just looked there, at my kid sleeping on that ratty-assed couch, and it was like, no, my kid doesn't have to live like this because of some crazed maniac, it isn't right. But, you know, it's like no matter what you do, it isn't right.

Faced with the threat of retaliation for leaving, limited financial resources, and inadequate housing alternatives, these women were unable to safely and successfully leave their batterers.

All of these women feel that "the system" offered them little aid. But Shannon believes that, as both a woman and an African-American, she faced additional obstacles in receiving help from a society ruled by people of different class, race, and gender. For Shannon, being poor, black and female insured that she would be stranded in her abusive relationship. Indeed, national statistics show that poor women, black women, and women living in urban areas suffer the highest rates of intimate violence.[145] Shannon was a member of all three groups. "I knew about shelters," Shannon says, "but not for battered women. I knew that there were shelters for women and children, but not in Roxbury, anyways. In Roxbury, dog shelters, yeah." According to Shannon, violence in the home was something her inner-city neighborhood chose to ignore:

> People see what's going on. They see you getting beat up in the streets, they hear your cries at night. Especially coming from Roxbury, nobody's going to help you.

---

[144] Walker, *The Battered Woman*, 47.
[145] Department of Justice, *Violence by Intimates*. According to this study, women between the ages of 16 and 24 also experience among the highest levels of abuse.

> That's domestic affairs, and they don't want to get involved in it. Or they might not know it's a domestic affair, they might think it's drugs or something, that's the first thing that comes to mind, drugs, drugs, drugs, coming from Roxbury, or black-on-black crime.

In addition, Shannon faced the issue of turning her abuser over to white men, outsiders to her community and her way of life:

> I mean, in Roxbury, you just don't call the police. Being a black woman, being a black man, you don't turn your man into the white man. You're labeled as a snitch, I'd have to watch my back again, hoping that nobody runs up against me, or he doesn't have nobody beat me up' or he doesn't beat me up himself. So you just don't do that type of thing in Roxbury. I don't care what the circumstances are. Whether it's an abusive situation, whether it's black on black crime, whatever, drugs, gambling, whatever, you just don't call the police, it doesn't work that way.

The women describe endless incidents in which their attempts to leave or seek help were thwarted by others. Ironically, those generally considered potential helpers proved to be ineffective or unsympathetic to their situations. And, as sociologists John Johnson and Kathleen Ferraro explain, "disbelief or an unsympathetic response from others tends to suppress a woman's belief that she has been victimized and encourages her to accept what has happened as normal."[146] Without any external acknowledgment of their victimization, these women were unable to gain the support, both emotional and material, that they required in order to successfully leave their batterers. Within their stories, three potential sources of assistance emerge as obstacles to their escape: the police, the courts, and their family and friends.

Lisa called the police so many times that they stopped responding. "They knew who I was before I told them who I was," she says.

> I had restraining orders, I called the police, I sought out a divorce. He was charged with breaking and entering, for coming after me with a hammer. He knocked through my door, and that's the time he knocked all my teeth out. But he was charged with armed assault, attempted murder, a lot of charges, and nothing happened. So you see, if a woman did that, she'd be in doing time, probably ten to fifteen years, 'cause those charges are heavy. And if it were a

---

[146] John M. Johnson and Kathleen J. Ferraro, "The Victimized Self: The Case of Battered Women," in *The Existential Self in Society*, ed. Joseph A. Kotawba and Andrea Fontana (Chicago: The University of Chicago Press, 1984), 122.

stranger who did that to me, it would be different. Just because he was my husband, it was O.K. that he did that to me. You know, if it was a stranger, it would be a normal process, but nothing happened to him.

Many of the women also speak of doctors who treated their injuries and then released them without inquiry.[147] In Patricia's story, the medical profession joined the police in failing to protect her from her abuser:

> One time, oh, he beat the shit out of me. Broke my nose, and when I went to the hospital, one doctor said to the other, "Come here, it's a perfect break!" Can you believe it? But anyway, I'm standing there, I've got blood pouring down my face, I'm in the driveway, Brian's standing right at the door, the police drive up, and I'm saying, "Arrest him, arrest him!" I mean, you're not going to be, "Oh yes, officer, he punched me in the face," very calmly. Of course, you're going to be a little . . . hysterical. I didn't want to use that word, God forbid, women and hysterical. But it was awful. I was a little upset, and I said, "I want him arrested, I want him arrested right now." And they were like, "Well, we can't arrest him, we didn't see him do anything." And I said, "Oh, so you think I did this to myself? You think I walked into a door?" And I'm screaming. And they said, "What, do *you* want to be arrested? We'll take *you* down to the station." I was off the deep end. And now they leave and I'm standing in the driveway, and there's Brian, and I think, Oh God, he's going to kill me now. I mean, I just called the cops on him, the ultimate sin. And he dragged me in the house and beat me twice as bad. Teaches you not to call the police, you know what I mean? I mean, if you can take a beating that bad and live through it, then you should count your blessings, because if you call the police, then you're probably going to be dead. What's your option there, what would you do, know what I mean?

---

[147] Elaine grew addicted to the painkillers doctors repeatedly prescribed for her injuries. For further discussion of the medical profession's history of ineffectiveness regarding domestic violence, and prescriptions for future treatment of battered women, see Allen D. Eisenberg and David A. Dillon, "Medico-Legal Aspects of Representing the Battered Woman," (1980) in *Representing Battered Women Who Kill*, ed. Sara Lee Johann and Frank Osanka, 35-46, and Angela Browne, "Violence against Women: Relevance for Medical Practitioners," *Journal of the American Medical Association*, 267 (1992): 3184-9.

These women were trapped. In attempting to gain help from the police and others, they risked severe retaliation from their batterers. "We're in this corner, and nobody's around to help us," Shannon says.

The women also describe repeated demands for help from the courts; they took out restraining orders that went unenforced, they sought protection after receiving threats to their lives. Elaine speaks about the numerous worthless restraining orders she obtained: "I never saved the papers. It was like toilet paper then, you know? It just proved that he shouldn't be near me, even though nobody enforced it. But I was still trying to do things the right way, hoping that some day they would be honored or enforced, or whatever." But the criminal justice system failed to protect these women, viewing domestic abuse as less serious than other crimes and following a policy in which action would only be taken after the batterer had committed a crime; in almost all cases, a police officer would need to witness that offense in order to make an arrest.[148] Patricia feels that this inaction on the part of the criminal justice system led her to take action herself:

> It's because the courts wouldn't help me, that's how I ended up here. No one believed he was going to kill me. No one believed it was going to happen. Even before the incident happened, I went down to the courts with my father. And I said, "Look, he's calling me up and he's saying he's going to kill me and my kid. You *have* to help me, you *have* to do something." And the guy sat back in his chair and he said, "Well, I'm sorry Ma'am, but we can't do anything until he actually does something." And I became hysterical. And I said, "So what, I have to wait until I'm found face down in the gutter, me and my kid? *Then* you'll do something? *Then* is when you're going to do something?"

Although they sought acknowledgment from the police and courts that the abuse was life-threatening, their fears were never validated. Elaine says, "We're talking about years of abuse. How rational is that? How rational was society to me? A stranger can't get away with assault and battery, but this guy, even though I'm married to him, turns into a stranger, can't get arrested." These women consistently received the message that they had to face the violence alone. Patricia feels that the criminal justice system must lead the way to change: "I don't care how much we talk, we can talk until

---

[148] Until the early 1980s, most police departments and courts treated domestic assaults as misdemeanors, which the police needed to witness in order to make an arrest. While these policies gradually changed to allow arrest in cases with probable cause, police often continued their previous non-intervention practices. As late as 1984, the Justice Department noted that failure to arrest batterers contributed to the problem of domestic violence. See Gillespie, 136-7, and the Department of Justice, *Final Report of the Attorney General's Task Force on Domestic Violence* (Washington, D.C., 1984), 11-2; 22-4.

we're blue in the face, the laws have got to be changed, and nothing's gonna be done until the laws have been changed. Not only changed, but enforced."

Along with the criminal justice system, the women turned to people close to them for assistance. But, as Shannon explains, despite her obvious injuries, her family chose to look away: "Sometimes I would walk around with two black eyes, and my family would ask me what happened, and I would tell them I walked into the door. And they had a sense, they knew what was going on." Shannon also explains that friends and neighbors feared that José's violence might turn on them: "You know, that's how it was with José, they would not mess with him. When José came or they heard his name, people walked the other way. They were terrified of him. He was violent with everybody."

Elaine also says that her attempts to confide in her friends and family met silence and denial. Those whom she trusted were unwilling to acknowledge the abuse or help her escape:

> I did [tell friends about the abuse] and it seemed like after I did, I felt like I was punished for it. Because people were like, "Oh, I don't want to hear that." That's probably what was going through their minds, and they'd stop calling, and I'd feel like I was punished for it, for saying something. I told some friends, some family members, and my mother was a battered woman, she was being battered, so to her it was normal, and I should live with it, try to make the best of it.
>
> I was going to get away, I was making it to get away, and I did. In '84, around March, I left again, and I took all my furniture from my apartment, and I put it down in my mother's basement. And one day I came home, and they had him in the house. And he had brought filet mignon, and hams, and money to make phone calls. He handed them 200 dollars in cash and said, "I have to make some phone calls." And it's: "I'm sorry, I'm sorry, please forgive me." And they acted just like I did when he first started on me, and they forgave him, just like I did the first time. I came in the house, and it was horrible to see him there, I felt betrayed.

This reaction from Elaine's parents echoes her own behavior during the initial stages of her relationship. Like her family, she wanted to forgive, to believe her batterer's promises to change. But long after Elaine had abandoned this hope, her family's efforts to preserve her marriage continued to frustrate her attempts to escape.

JUSTICE

These four women tell similar stories of abuse and thwarted attempts to leave. Yet, although their actions share a context of victimization, their accounts of killing differ. All of these women feel morally culpable for their batterers' deaths; however, they also feel various degrees of legal accountability for their actions. Their stories highlight the complex definitions of justice for battered women who kill and the need for individualized evaluation of their cases by the criminal justice system.

All of these women believed that they would eventually be killed by their abusers. Often, they prepared themselves: "Before all of this happened," Elaine says, "I was writing a will out, giving all of my stuff away. I planned for my death." The danger was clear; they knew their batterers' capacity for violence. They felt that death was inevitable — either their abusers' or their own. "It's like a cat being cornered," Shannon says. "A person can take but so much, and a cat can take but so much before he attacks and knows that he has nowhere to move and he's going to defend himself, before his life is taken. And that's how we are."

Nonetheless, all of the women express tremendous regret at taking a life. Their feelings concerning their claims of self-defense are extremely complicated; in defending themselves against attackers, they also killed men they loved. "And to this day I still have love for him," Shannon says, "because it's like a part of me died with him."

Elaine and Shannon killed their abusers during battering incidents; they believe that they acted in direct response to a life-threatening danger. Shannon explains: "It was nothing that was premeditated, or something I planned, it just happened. He pulled the gun out on me, and I ended up taking it, and I ended up shooting him with it."

Most of the women did not know they had killed their abusers until they were arrested for murder. For example, Shannon fled the scene to avoid further injury, believing that José had only been hurt. Elaine lost consciousness during the incident: "the whole thing happened so fast. In one second, I was defending myself. I didn't even know what I had grabbed, because he had cornered me and I was just trying to stop him." To this day she has difficulty recalling the details of the homicide. "I know I struck him," Elaine says, "but I never got to see what was in my hand. Because I was going off the ground, I struck him and he threw me against the wall. But I look at it like this: I'm doing the time, I better have done it."

Elaine and Shannon believe that only a pardon would be an adequate outcome of their cases. Although they feel moral guilt over killing, they also feel legally innocent of murder. They believe that their actions constituted reasonable and justified self-defense; they deserve to be exonerated through the clemency process, as they should have been within a court of law. "I would further pursue [my commutation appeal] with a pardon," Elaine says. "I feel that God has forgiven me, I've forgiven myself. I didn't deserve to be beat all those years. I should be exonerated with a full governor's pardon. I don't even want to hear about it.

Exonerate me." Shannon agrees that a pardon would offer her the only opportunity for true freedom and justice:

> I'm the one that suffered. I went through all the turmoil and everything. I'm the one that got beaten every day, every night, four or five times a day. I've already asked God to forgive me, and that's the only person I need to ask. And I don't feel that people should go on judging me. I want my case overturned. I don't want them walking behind me, watching my every move. I'm still in prison that way. I want a pardon, yeah.

But Patricia and Lisa's cases differ from these other two women who claim justified self-defense. Both Patricia and Lisa were divorced at the time of the homicides, and they did not kill their batterers during physical confrontations. Unlike Elaine and Shannon, Patricia and Lisa believe that they did deserve some punishment, but not the severe sentences they received. Commutation, they feel, would be a suitable remedy for their unjust treatment throughout the trial process.

Interestingly, Patricia and Lisa feel that their actions were unjustified, morally and legally. They stress the fact that they are not innocent. "As bad as he was," Patricia says, "it doesn't mean that I had a right to take a life. Some days, I think that if I could have him back alive, I'd take a beating from him every day, rather than feel like I feel about taking his life. It was awful that it had to happen like that." Patricia says that, at the time, she felt shooting her ex-husband to protect herself and her son was her only option. She felt trapped, and she knew that someone was going to die:

> I remember it, exactly, like it was yesterday. I remember, right before it happened, that feeling, and I felt it right down to my soul, and I was panicked. I didn't know what to do, I was like a little caged dog, it was like that sort of thing. I felt like, I mean, the whole thing was really heavy, it was like I was caught up in fate, like this was destined to happen, him or me. It was going to be one of us, and there was no turning back and there was no other way for it to happen. And then afterwards, I remember thinking, it was insane, I must have been temporarily insane. But, you know, there's a very fine line between sanity and insanity. And I was walking it. But, now that I look back on it, and I'm feeling better about myself, I think the insane part was putting up with the abuse for all these years. The sanest thing I ever did was to defend my life.

Although Patricia does not feel that her behavior was irrational, she believes that she was wrong to kill. Patricia believes that a reduction of her sentence would be more appropriate than a pardon in her situation:

> I never said it was an accident, that the gun misfired. I'm saying, "Yeah, I shot the gun and killed him, but the reasons that it happened are this." It was either him or me. I'm not asking to be found not guilty, because I am guilty, I took his life, I did it. But, there were extenuating circumstances, and they should take that into consideration, you know. A pardon is not guilty, commutation isn't. I am definitely guilty of taking his life, I mean, if I was found not guilty, they'd have to look for who did it, right, I mean, someone's got to be guilty. And I certainly take responsibility for what I did, I have no problem with that, but I certainly don't deserve 18 to 20 years for it.

Lisa is the only woman who did not kill her abuser herself. Two male friends, having witnessed Tom assaulting her, offered to help. Lisa did not learn that Tom had been killed until the following day, when the police arrived to arrest her. Though Lisa takes responsibility for her batterer's death, she also feels that her punishment was incommensurate with her role in the homicide. "I believe that I should do some time," Lisa says, "but I've done eight years. To me, that's plenty — way beyond plenty." Like Patricia, she believes that the circumstances of the event should be considered:

> I do take responsibility for my actions. I have to. I mean, there was a death. Not that I planned there to be a death, but it ended up that he died, when he was beat up. And I can't change that, nothing I can do can change that fact. And I've done eight years in prison because of it. But in my fight, I just want them to realize what happened to *me* in that relationship.

Lisa emphasizes that although she is morally culpable for her batterer's death, she also deserves another evaluation of her legal responsibility for the event: "Nobody should die, of any reason, women especially, in a battering situation. If they've got paper trails behind them, and people aren't listening, and something happens and she kills him, then they need to look at the whole picture."

Although Lisa and Patricia do state that they should be partially excused based on their past abuse, they also believe that their behavior was understandable given their situations. They do not attempt to justify their behavior, but they ask that the context of their actions be considered. Elaine and Shannon, on the other hand, feel that they acted in self-defense, in direct response to their abusers' lethal violence. Both women believe that exoneration of guilt though a full pardon by the governor would be most just.

The stories of these four women reveal the complex meanings of their acts — their cases defy general categorization. The women differ in the perceptions of their behavior, the punishments they feel they deserve, and the forms of clemency they seek. They themselves believe that their actions require individual evaluation. Their claims fall within a continuum of justification and excuse, and acknowledging this is crucial to adequate treatment of their cases. Yet one theme does run through their stories: they believe that clemency should be considered an act of equity, rather than mercy, in their cases — they are not seeking forgiveness, but justice. They have all been victims, yet they have also acted as survivors. None of these women argue that they should be excused because the abuse made them helpless or irrational. They emphasize the circumstances of their actions, urging the criminal justice system to look at the violence they endured, at their inability to separate from their batterers, and at the lack of resources or solutions offered to them. The mitigating factors they stress are their batterers' violence and society's unwillingness to help, not an impaired perception of alternatives to homicide. Whether they feel their behavior was justified or not, the circumstances of their actions deserve full consideration, for only then will justice be possible.

CONCLUSION

I have attempted to address several questions in this book. Does the battered woman syndrome adequately describe the experiences of battered women who kill? Do existing challenges to the theory suggest more suitable explanations for these women's actions? Can the life stories of the women themselves provide new definitions of their situations? Finally, what constitutes justice in battered women's self-defense cases, and can this determination produce more effective responses to battered women in the future?

Both society and its legal system rely on categories to judge the behavior of individuals. Often, however, these classifications are too narrow and fail to account for the complexity of human experience. The battered woman syndrome represents an attempt to describe the perspectives of battered women as reasonable within a subjective framework of self-defense law. But instead of strengthening the voices of women who have killed their abusers, this theory may actually disempower them by inadequately representing their experiences. Elizabeth Schneider has effectively argued that the use of a "syndrome" to describe the perceptions and actions of a battered woman is dangerous, for it implies that the woman is damaged or abnormal, suffering from a disease or pathological disorder. The battered woman syndrome fails to properly consider the circumstances of her behavior. Furthermore, in focusing on the woman's inaction, the theory does not adequately address, and may even contradict, the reasonableness of her final defensive act. The battered woman syndrome works to preclude a determination of justified self-defense before it is fairly considered.

Although Elizabeth Schneider and other feminist legal scholars recognize dilemmas in using the battered woman syndrome to describe women who kill their abusers, they do not suggest that advocates and attorneys abandon this category: "The problem is that there's a tilt in the way [the battered woman syndrome] is heard. But we still need expert testimony on the battered woman syndrome in court,"[149] Schneider argues. Despite the fact that it is susceptible to misuse and misinterpretation, legal theorists such as Schneider stress that the syndrome theory has helped

---

[149] Elizabeth Schneider, telephone conversation with author, 6 October 1993.

dispel common misconceptions concerning battered women's behavior. I argue, however, that an essential aspect of the theory is incorrect; even careful articulation of the battered woman syndrome will not remedy its shortcomings. By focusing on the psychology of battered women, the theory draws attention away from the real external forces that shape their behavior. If a "syndrome" does exist, it lies within the batterers who execute the violence and the society that tolerates it.

The stories of women who have killed their abusers do suggest that a descriptive theory is useful and even essential for understanding their experiences. The concepts of domestic violence and the battered woman syndrome have connected their individual life stories to those of other women, validating their past victimization and redefining them as survivors. But their accounts also reveal a disparity between the theory of the battered woman syndrome and the reality of these women's lives. Although the women embrace the concept of the cycle of violence, learned helplessness — the element most frequently highlighted by the legal and psychological communities — is inconsistent with their experiences. The syndrome has constructed a category of helplessness that rejects the survival behavior of these women. Helplessness certainly exists in their stories, but only in the context of very real obstacles, such as their batterers' retaliation and concrete social and legal barriers to their safe separation. The concept of learned helplessness suggests that the route to escape is open, and that battered women only perceive barriers. I argue that the real cages restraining these women must be examined and eliminated.

These women's stories suggest that a reformulated theory of domestic violence should highlight at least two elements: the behavior of the batterer and the reaction of society's traditional help-providers to the woman's escape efforts. One aspect of Walker's theory, the cycle of violence, should be included in this picture. This concept describes the escalating abuse a woman faces in a battering relationship, explaining her final action as a reaction to her batterer's life-threatening attacks.

The women's stories also suggest separation assault as a necessary instrument for viewing their behavior. This theory examines the real physical threat that prevents a woman from successfully leaving an abusive relationship. Like the cycle of violence, the notion of separation assault concentrates on the batterer's abusive behavior rather than on the woman's psychological state to explain her actions.

Finally, this revised theory must include a discussion of society's indifference in the face of domestic abuse. If the police had arrested Patricia's husband, if the courts had enforced Lisa's restraining orders, and if Shannon's family had acknowledged her injuries, perhaps their batterers would not be dead and the women would not be in prison today. Traditional sources of assistance consistently failed to offer these women any alternatives to living in violence.

The theory emerging from these narratives describes battered women as active survivors of life-threatening circumstances. The notions of the cycle of violence, separation assault, and society's indifference focus on the context of a battered woman's behavior. Unlike learned helplessness, these concepts are compatible with a battered woman's experiences and logical in relation to her legal defense: they account for both her victimization and her agency in the situation. In addition, a theory combining these elements will not require a "reasonable battered woman" standard for a determination of self-defense. Focusing on the circumstances of a homicide, juries may conclude that any reasonable individual might have acted in justified self-defense. The battered woman must no longer be excused in order to gain her freedom.

This social theory of domestic violence can explain that battered women face similar external constraints in attempting to escape from their abusers, but it should not imply that their acts of killing are identical. Despite their similarities, the women's accounts reveal significant differences among the cases of battered women who kill, differences that the criminal justice system must consider in judging these acts. All of the women believe that their voices have been silenced throughout the legal process. The danger they faced was never articulated in the courtroom. When they do tell their stories, however, it becomes clear that they feel various degrees of accountability for the killings. Patricia and Lisa, for example, say that they take responsibility for their actions and acknowledge society's need for retribution. An injustice has been committed in these women's eyes. However, it does not lie in their convictions, but in the harshness of their punishments. On the other hand, Elaine and Shannon feel that they should have been acquitted — they believe that they acted in justified self-defense. For these two women, commutations will not be adequate; they believe that only pardons will yield justice in their cases.

I do not suggest that these women's actions should be judged according to their personal conceptions of moral and legal accountability. As I have stated, these women have much at stake in presenting their cases in the manner most likely to secure their freedom. However, the women's own perceptions of their behavior can inform society's notion of justice in these cases. Instead of viewing women's acts through disempowering, narrow categories such as the battered woman syndrome, the law must begin to take individual differences into account within the framework of a social theory of domestic violence. Battered women who have killed are still prevented from receiving equity: the courts preclude them from presenting their actions as justifiable, and the extra-judicial process of clemency often fails to offer them the opportunity to be pardoned. Excuse within the courts and commutation within clemency may be a suitable determination and gesture for some, but not all, battered women who kill.

Although I have focused on the stories of battered women who have killed, I believe that the lessons derived from their experiences extend beyond these specific cases. An examination of the social forces and legal obstacles women face in leaving can lead to more equitable treatment of battered women's self-defense cases. But it can also suggest ways in which social and legal institutions should respond to those women who have yet to act, or who may never act at all. "I don't want other women to end up like me," Lisa says. "Death is not the answer, of her or him. So you have to give the women the support to do the right thing. You have to give them the support and the information they need." These women's stories reveal a failure to understand and effectively treat the problem of domestic violence as a whole. Only when we recognize the real barriers women face in escaping abusive relationships will we begin to ask appropriate questions and seek suitable solutions. Before challenging the battered woman's behavior, members of the criminal justice system and the rest of society must begin to examine our own.

EPILOGUE

THE BATTERED WOMAN SYNDROME: FIVE YEARS LATER

Scientific knowledge in the area of domestic violence has increased dramatically since I began this project in the Spring of 1993. At that time, the battered woman syndrome was the accepted theory for describing the psychological and behavioral reactions of women to intimate abuse. As this book has discussed, the psychiatric and legal communities embraced this tool as a means of explaining battered women's behavior to the public and, in particular, to juries and governors judging their claims of self-defense.

In the last few years, the psychiatric community has begun to distance itself from the concept of learned helplessness in describing battered women. Indeed, Martin Seligman himself has stated that its application to battered women is a misinterpretation of his original theory. In 1993, he and his colleagues wrote:

> We think that the passivity observed among victims of domestic violence is a middling example of learned helplessness. Passivity is present, but it may well be instrumental. Cognitions of helplessness are present, as is a history of uncontrollability. But there may also be a history of *explicit reinforcement for passivity*. Taken together, *these results do not constitute the best possible support for concluding that these women show learned helplessness*. (Italics added)[150]

---

[150] Christopher Peterson, Steven F. Maier, Martin E. P. Seligman, *Learned Helplessness: A Theory for the Age of Personal Control* (New York: Oxford University Press, 1993), 239.

In other words, there are very real bars to the cages that contain these women. Their helplessness, where it exists, may be largely in reaction to social, legal, and economic rather than solely psychological barriers.

Members of the criminal justice system also have begun to move away from the descriptively inaccurate and legally restrictive concept of learned helplessness. In 1996, the U.S. Congress asked a group of state and federal judges, prosecutors, and defense attorneys to prepare a report on the impact of expert testimony on domestic violence in criminal cases.[151] In discussing the battered woman syndrome, this report advised that "the term does not incorporate the breadth of available knowledge concerning battering and its effects that may be relevant in a criminal case involving a battered woman."[152] The report called for an expansion of expert testimony to include more current and comprehensive theories, observations, and empirical findings on the effects of domestic violence. "A more accurate representation of battering and its effects includes a range of issues on the nature and dynamics of battering, the effects of violence, battered women's responses to violence, and the social and psychological context in which domestic violence occurs . . . . Such testimony that derives from the body of scientific knowledge is more useful to the factfinder than dated or stereotypic notions of battered women as *passive or helpless*," (italics added)[153] the panel concluded. According to these judges and attorneys, the battered woman syndrome is not only inadequate to describe her experiences, but it can "potentially mislead the factfinder in consideration of a criminal matter involving a battered woman."[154] Careful articulation of the battered woman syndrome is not the solution. Both the scientific and the legal communities now agree that the battered woman syndrome should be abandoned in light of current knowledge about battered women's experiences and their responses to violence.

POSTTRAUMATIC STRESS DISORDER

While there is now general acknowledgment that a theory focusing on learned helplessness is inconsistent with battered women's behavior and

---

[151] Both this report and a report by Janet Parrish (see note 24) responded to a requirement for information in the 1994 Violence Against Women Act (VAWA), Title IV of the Violent Crime Control and Law Enforcement Act (P.L. 103-322).

[152] Mary Ann Dutton, "Impact of Evidence Concerning Battering and Its Effects in Criminal Trials Involving Battered Women," in *The Validity and Use of Evidence Concerning Battering and its Effects in Criminal Trials,* Report Responding to Section 40507 of the Violence Against Women Act (Washington, D.C.: U.S. Department of Justice and U.S. Department of Health and Human Services, May 1996, NCJ 160972), 5.

[153] Ibid., 5.

[154] Ibid., 6.

their legal claims, there is no doubt that women can experience severe psychological harm from a partner's abuse. Recently, clinicians and researchers have begun to examine the rapidly expanding literature on reactions to trauma for insight into the effects of violence on women.

Studies have shown that battered women share some experiences and responses with other trauma survivors. In 1984, researcher Angela Browne noted that "with all types of trauma, whether related to a natural disaster, war, or a more personal offense, the fear is of a force that has been out of control."[155] Battered women, according to Browne, are much like victims of torture or repeated unpredictable disasters; these individuals may develop psychological symptoms that continue long after the original event. This response is known as Posttraumatic Stress Disorder (PTSD). According to the *Diagnostic and Statistical Manual of Mental Disorders*, or the DSM-IV, as the primary psychiatric diagnostic text is commonly known, PTSD is characterized by "*an extreme traumatic stressor* involving direct personal experience of an event that involves actual or threatened death or serious injury, or other threat to one's personal integrity." (Italics added)[156] In addition, the person must react to the event itself with "intense fear, helplessness, or horror."[157] Symptoms of PTSD may include reexperiencing of the traumatic event; avoidance of reminders of the event and general emotional numbing; and increased arousal or hypervigilance.[158]

Originally developed to describe the psychological symptoms and flashbacks of Vietnam War veterans, some experts have argued that Posttraumatic Stress Disorder fits the cognitive, behavioral, and emotional processes exhibited by some abused women.[159] A 1985 study by Romero compared men who had been prisoners of war with a sample of battered women. The study found that both groups had experienced damaging psychological abuse; dependency on their abusers and isolation from others; and episodes of support from their abusers that reinforced their reliance on the captors.[160] These elements are similar to Lenore Walker's description of the cycle of violence that operates within battering relationships.

---

[155] Browne, *When Battered Women Kill*, 124. For early comparisons between battered women and victims of torture, see Walker, *The Battered Woman*, 49; Walker, *Terrifying Love*, 48; Browne, *When Battered Women Kill*, 124-5; and *State v. Hundley*, 236 Kan. 461, 693 P.2d 475 (1985).

[156] American Psychiatric Association, *Diagnostic and Statistical Manual of Mental Disorders*, 4th ed. (Washington, D.C: Author, 1994), 424.

[157] Ibid., 424.

[158] Ibid.

[159] Walker, *Terrifying Love*, n. 48.

[160] Mary Romero, "A Comparison between Strategies Used on Prisoners of War and Abused Wives," *Sex Roles* 13 (1985): 537-47. For a discussion of battered women's psychological reactions to trauma, see Koss et al., 74-94;

In fact, Walker herself eventually linked the battered woman syndrome to the concept of PTSD. "The diagnosis of battered woman syndrome as a subcategory of PTSD is probably the most prevalent manifestation of psychological trauma from living with repeated violence,"[161] she wrote in 1991. Walker also acknowledged advantages in using PTSD over the narrower battered woman syndrome to describe abused women. Significantly, she recognized both "political and clinical reasons that support the use of the diagnostic category of PTSD with battered women... PTSD stresses the abnormal nature of the stressor which causes the mental health symptoms, not individual pathology."[162]

However, Walker and other researchers have noted that battered women may develop symptoms from their particular traumatic experiences that differ from those of combat veterans, for example. "Like in other subclassifications of PTSD that measure dysfunction following repeated man-made trauma," Walker explains, "there are different symptom patterns observable in addition to the core group of arousal, avoidance, and intrusive cognitive memories present in a PTSD."[163] Yet Walker still holds tenaciously to her concept of learned helplessness as one of those symptoms that make battered women unique.[164]

When I interviewed the four women in 1993, the application of a traumatic stress theory to battered women was still quite recent; there had been little systematic study of PTSD among battered women in general, let alone among battered women who had killed. While I did not analyze the women's accounts for elements of this theory, in retrospect, their stories may contain some PTSD indications. Fear, terror, flashbacks of abuse, and feelings of helplessness could all be considered posttraumatic stress symptoms.

Only a few studies using standardized PTSD measures have since been conducted with battered women. The results, however, have been eye-opening. Rates of PTSD have ranged from 33 percent to 58 percent among community samples of abused women, and up to 84 percent among battered women in shelters.[165] A 1998 study compared rates of PTSD

---

[161] Lenore Walker, "Post-Traumatic Stress Disorder in Women: Diagnosis and Treatment of Battered Woman Syndrome," *Psychotherapy* 28.1 (Spring 1991): 22.
[162] Ibid., 22
[163] Ibid., 21.
[164] Ibid., 21-2.
[165] See Millie C. Astin, Kathy J. Lawrence, and David W. Foy, "Posttraumatic Stress Disorder among Battered Women: Risk and Resiliency Factors," *Violence and Victims* 8.1 (1993): 17-28; Millie C. Astin et al., "Posttraumatic Stress Disorder and Childhood Abuse in Battered Women: Comparisons with Maritally Distressed Women," *Journal of Consulting and Clinical Psychology* 64.2 (1995): 308-12; Beth M. Houskamp and David W. Foy, "The Assessment of Posttraumatic Stress Disorder in Battered Women," *Journal of Interpersonal Violence* 6.3 (1991): 367-75; and Anita Kemp, Edna I. Rawlings, and Bonnie L. Green, "Post-Traumatic Stress Disorder in Battered Women: A Shelter Sample," *Journal of Traumatic Stress* 4.1 (1991): 137-48.

among women imprisoned for killing their abusers and battered women incarcerated for other crimes. The researcher found that about half of the women in both groups had symptoms severe enough to meet the criteria for PTSD.[166]

These findings highlight several important points. First, prolonged abuse at the hands of a partner can have severe psychological consequences for women. Second, battered women may experience psychological reactions that are similar to victims of other traumatic events. PTSD provides a useful framework for understanding the psychological effects of battering because it focuses on the traumatic event itself. Unlike the battered woman syndrome and learned helplessness, PTSD emphasizes the captivity of abused women. In addition, by linking these women to other trauma survivors, this theory portrays their reactions as understandable and valid.

PTSD also offers a valuable prescription for guiding the psychological treatment of battered women. Women suffering from PTSD need supportive services that specifically address the traumatic nature of their experience. For while some battered women may have substance abuse or other problems in addition to PTSD, research shows that drug treatment alone, for example, will not effectively alleviate trauma-related symptoms such as avoidance of event reminders or emotional numbing.[167]

Finally, although battered women's experiences may be like those of other victims, we need further research on how the specific symptomatology of abused women might differ from that of other trauma survivors. For even an analogy between battered women and prisoners of war is not satisfactory. Battered women do undergo repeated trauma within a state of imprisonment, but, unlike most hostages, they have known their abusers intimately. Furthermore, battered women may still be enduring the violence, or they may be separated but living in constant fear of retaliation. These distinctions are significant; the theory of Posttraumatic Stress Disorder requires further expansion to describe the specific psychological effects of relationship abuse on human beings in general, and on women in particular.

Yet, regardless of PTSD's descriptive and therapeutic utility, it is no more appropriate than the battered woman syndrome to a woman's claim of justified self-defense. Introducing a diagnosis of PTSD in a courtroom or clemency proceeding would create the same legal trap by focusing on the abused woman's psychological impairment rather the external dangers and obstacles she has faced. A woman pleading justified self-defense must demonstrate that her perception of imminent, life-threatening danger was understandable. To that end, domestic violence experts can help bolster her claims by presenting her specific experiences within the context of

---

[166] Maura O'Keefe, "Posttraumatic Stress Disorder among Battered Women: A Comparison of Battered Women Who Killed Their Abusers and Those Incarcerated for Other Offenses," *Journal of Traumatic Stress* 11.1 (1998): 71-85.
[167] Koss et al., 92.

more general theories such as the cycle of violence, separation assault, and society's indifference to domestic abuse. Juries should be able to deduce from a woman's history of assaults from her batterer, and from the existing social, economic, and legal barriers to her successful escape, whether her fear of future attacks was reasonable. Rarely, however, should a psychiatric diagnosis such as PTSD be relevant to a battered woman's claim of justified self-defense.

RATES OF DOMESTIC VIOLENCE – THE CURRENT PICTURE

According to federal statistics, murder by intimates has decreased significantly in the past two decades.[168] In 1996, the latest year for which figures are available, there were approximately 1,800 intimate murders in this country – down 36 percent from the nearly 3,000 recorded in 1976.

Spouse murder, the largest component of these crimes, fell 52 percent over this period. The Department of Justice attributes this overall decline to a substantial drop in the number of violent domestic crimes committed with guns. Since 1976, intimate murders with firearms have decreased by about 10 percent, although in 1996, most intimate murders — 61 percent — were still committed with guns.

While this overall decline in partner homicide is certainly good news, closer inspection reveals that it is primarily due to a sharp drop in the rate of male intimate murder victims. The rate of female victims has remained relatively stable over the past two decades. Each year, thirty percent of all

---

[168] Department of Justice, Bureau of Justice Statistics, *Violence by Intimates: Analysis of Data on Crimes by Current or Former Spouses, Boyfriends, and Girlfriends* (Washington, D.C., March 1998, NCJ 167237). All data on intimate violence in this Epilogue, unless otherwise noted, is based on the above publication. This report is a compilation of statistical data from the Bureau of Justice Statistics (BJS) and the Federal Bureau of Investigation (FBI) on violence between intimates, who generally include current or former spouses, same sex partners, boyfriends, and girlfriends. Violent offenses encompass crimes such as murder, rape, sexual assault, robbery, aggravated assault, and simple assault. (Murder includes nonnegligent manslaughter). The data come from several sources. The National Crime Victimization Survey (NCVS) gathers statistics on criminal victimization from a national sample of household respondents. In addition, two components of the FBI's Uniform Crime Reporting Program (UCR), the National Incident-Based Reporting Program (NIBRS) and the Supplementary Homicide Reports (SHR), provide information from police on the victim-offender relationship in violent crimes. The Study of Injured Victims of Violence collects data on intentional injuries brought to the attention of hospital personnel. Finally, BJS also conducts national surveys of prison inmates, including details about the offender's relationship to the victim and how the crime was carried out.

female homicide victims are killed by a partner.[169] In 1996, three out of every four victims of intimate murder were women.

However, the number of female victims of *non-lethal* intimate violence has declined over the past few years. While women experienced approximately 1.1 million sexual attacks, robberies, and assaults at the hands of a partner in 1993, that number had decreased to 840,000 in 1996. Still, compared to men, women experience a much higher proportion of violence committed by a partner or spouse. Approximately 21 percent of violent crimes against women are committed by an intimate, compared to two percent of the violence sustained by men.

Increasingly, women are reporting these crimes to the authorities, and the authorities are taking stronger action. In 1996, women reported about one half of all incidents of partner violence to the police — a significant increase since 1973.[170] In 60 percent of these cases, according to the victims, the police arrived within 10 minutes; in about 20 percent of the reported incidents, police immediately arrested the batterer at the scene.[171]

There are also signs that the punishment for domestic violence is growing commensurate with the penalty for violence outside the home. According to the federal government, in 1996, the average prison sentence for harming an intimate was comparable to that for similar crimes against strangers. Inmates convicted of assaulting their spouses actually received longer sentences than those who assaulted strangers. Currently, about 25 percent of inmates in local jails and about seven percent of state prisoners are serving time for violence against a partner.

THE FEDERAL RESPONSE TO PARTNER VIOLENCE

The federal government recently has taken unprecedented steps to combat domestic violence in this country. In 1994, President Clinton signed the Violence Against Women Act (VAWA).[172] The law addresses rape and sexual assault, domestic violence, women's legal rights, and protections for battered immigrant women and children. These measures combine strong new penalties for domestic violence with programs to assist victims and raise public awareness about partner violence.

Through this legislation, states have received resources to hire more prosecutors for domestic crimes and improve training on battering and its effects for police officers, prosecutors, judges. In addition, the law makes tracking victims across state lines a federal offense. It also requires states

---

[169] Overall, the number of intimate murders has decreased by five percent each year for male victims, but just one percent for female victims, since 1976.

[170] Reports to the police have increased about three percent each year since 1993.

[171] As reported by female victims of intimate violence.

[172] The Violence Against Women Act (VAWA) is Title IV of the Violent Crime Control and Law Enforcement Act (P.L. 103-322).

to honor restraining orders against batterers issued in other states; makes it illegal for anyone under a restraining order to possess a firearm; and grants victims mandatory restitution and the right to address the court at their batterers' sentencing.

Finally, VAWA provided funding for more shelters, counseling services, and research into domestic violence treatment and prevention. It created a 24-hour national hotline, which, since its launch in February 1996, has received over 150,000 calls. The majority of these calls are from women who have never before reached out for help.[173]

BATTERED WOMEN'S SELF-DEFENSE – FIVE YEARS LATER

When members of the Framingham Eight went on trial in the mid-1980s, only Lisa Grimshaw was allowed to introduce expert testimony on battering and its effects. However, within the last few years, courts across the United States have increasingly recognized the relevance of expert testimony to support battered women's self-defense claims.

Recently, the U.S. Congress requested an analysis of the extent to which evidence and expert testimony on domestic violence has been admitted in criminal trials since the mid-1980s. The responding report, prepared by the National Clearinghouse for the Defense of Battered Women, was based on an analysis of 238 state court decisions, 31 federal court decisions, and 12 state statutes. The study found that expert testimony on battering and its effects is now admissible, at least to some degree, in all 50 states and the District of Columbia. In the 19 federal courts that have considered the issue, 16 have admitted expert testimony. In addition, 12 states, including Massachusetts, have actually enacted statutes supporting the admissibility of expert testimony on battering and its effects within criminal trials.[174]

However, introducing expert testimony on domestic violence in court does not guarantee a "not guilty" verdict for a battered woman defendant. The same study examined the appeals of 152 battered women defendants in state courts. It found that 32 percent of these cases were reversed on appeal, and of these cases, 45 percent were reversed based on erroneous exclusion of, limitation of, or failure of counsel to present expert testimony on domestic violence. Thus, overall, just 14 percent of the 152 cases were reversed on grounds related to erroneous exclusion of expert

---

[173] Department of Health and Human Services, *Preventing Violence Against Women*, factsheet (Washington, D.C., May 1998).

[174] Janet Parrish, "Trend Analysis: Expert Testimony on Battering and its Effects in Criminal Cases," in *The Validity and Use of Evidence Concerning Battering and its Effects in Criminal Trials,* Report Responding to Section 40507 of the Violence Against Women Act (Washington, D.C.: U.S. Department of Justice and U.S. Department of Health and Human Services, May 1996, NCJ 160972), 2-3.

testimony. Significantly, 71 percent of the convictions that were affirmed on appeal by higher courts had admitted or found admissible expert testimony on battering and its effects.[175] In other words, although expert testimony was used or recognized by the court in most of these appellate cases, the women's convictions were nonetheless upheld. As the report notes, "This is strong evidence that — contrary to popular misconceptions reflected in some media coverage of this issue — the defense's use of or the court's awareness about expert testimony on battering in no way equates to acquittal on the criminal charges lodged against a battered woman defendant."[176] In recent years, some legal scholars and members of the public have argued that introducing stories of their past abuse would lead to a wave of acquittals for battered women who killed – research on these cases shows otherwise.[177]

THE WOMEN'S STORIES: FIVE YEARS LATER

Five years have passed since I originally interviewed Shannon, Lisa, Patricia, and Elaine in prison. In some ways, not much has changed. Although Governor Weld eventually commuted the sentences of two members of the original Framingham Eight, he did not grant clemency to any of the four women I interviewed.

Shannon Booker was paroled from prison in 1994. She immediately began to speak out about domestic violence, instructing high school students, hospital workers, and police officers to learn from her own experiences. She spoke at a United Nations summit in Copenhagen with First Lady Hillary Rodham Clinton. Meanwhile, however, she continued to fight her longstanding battle with depression and substance abuse. In 1997, Shannon entered another abusive relationship. Within a few months, she was charged with violating her parole for theft. After a three-day trial, the judge hearing her case found Shannon not guilty by reason of insanity. A psychiatrist had testified that Shannon suffered from depression, experienced hallucinations, and had heard the voice of José, the abuser she killed. Following further psychiatric evaluation, Shannon will either return to the Framingham prison to serve the remainder of her original 1990 sentence, or be sent to a state mental hospital for treatment.[178]

Lisa Grimshaw was granted parole in 1993. She achieved her goal of educating others, training Massachusetts law enforcement officers in

---

[175] Ibid., 36-7.
[176] Ibid., 37.
[177] See Alan M. Dershowitz, *The Abuse Excuse* (Boston: Little, Brown and Company, 1994).
[178] John Ellement, "Judge Rules Framingham Eight Member Insane when She Stole," *The Boston Globe*, 20 March 1998, A1.

domestic violence issues. In March 1998, Lisa was arrested for violating her parole and was ordered back to MCI Framingham.

Elaine Hyde was released on parole in 1994. She returned to school, receiving her B.A. degree in Women's Studies from Boston College in 1996. Elaine hopes one day to pursue a law degree and ultimately secure pardons for herself and other battered women convicted of killing their abusers.

Patricia Hennessy's requests for both clemency and early parole have been repeatedly denied. She continues to live at MCI Lancaster, serving the remainder of her original 18- to 20-year sentence.

JUSTICE: FIVE YEARS LATER

Since 1993, approximately 37 incarcerated battered women have received clemency in the United States. Most of these women have had their sentences commuted; three were pardoned. However, because governors and pardon boards are not required to explain the reasons for their decisions, it is difficult to state with certainty that all of these women received clemency based on their past histories of abuse. For example, for some governors, an incarcerated woman's physical illness or disability may have been a more salient factor in granting clemency than her past victimization. Nonetheless, although we lack current national estimates of their appeals, women across the country continue to seek clemency based on their battering experiences.[179] They join Patricia Hennessy in Massachusetts, who still seeks freedom.

---

[179] National Clearinghouse for the Defense of Battered Women, "Battered Women Who Have Received Clemency: 1978-1996," draft report, Philadelphia, PA, January 1998.

BIBLIOGRAPHY

BOOKS

American Psychiatric Association. *Diagnostic and Statistical Manual of Mental Disorders.* 4th ed. Washington, D.C: Author, 1994.

Browne, Angela. *When Battered Women Kill.* New York: The Free Press, 1987.

Campbell, Jacquelyn. *Nursing Assessment for Risk of Homicide with Battered Women.* Aspen: Aspen Publishers, 1986.

De Beauvoir, Simone. *The Second Sex.* New York: Knopf, 1952.

Deegan, Mary Jo and Michael Hill, eds. Introduction. *Women and Symbolic Interaction.* Boston: Allen & Unwin, Inc., 1987.

Denzin, Norman. *Interpretive Biography.* Newbury Park, CA: Sage Publications, 1989.

———. *The Research Act: A Theoretical Introduction to Sociological Methods.* New Jersey: Prentice Hall, 1989.

Dershowitz, Alan M. *The Abuse Excuse.* Boston: Little, Brown, and Company, 1994.

Dobash, R. Emerson and Russell Dobash. *Violence against Wives: A Case against the Patriarchy.* New York: The Free Press, 1979.

Dutton, Mary Ann. *Empowering and Healing the Battered Woman: A Model for Assessment and Intervention.* New York: Springer Publishing, 1992.

Ewing, Charles. *Battered Women Who Kill: Psychological Self-Defense as Legal Justification.* Lexington, MA: Lexington Books, 1987.

Feinman, Clarice. *Women in the Criminal Justice System.* New York: Preager, 1986.

Fraser, Kimberly. *Defending the Battered Woman Who Kills.* Paper Submitted for LLM Degree, Harvard University, 1991.

Gillespie, Cynthia. *Justifiable Homicide.* Columbus: Ohio State University Press, 1989.

Glaser, Barney and Anselm Strauss. *The Discovery of Grounded Theory: Strategies for Qualitative Research.* New York: Aldine Publishing Co., 1967.

Gondolf, Edward W. and Ellen R. Fisher. *Battered Women as Survivors: An Alternative to Treating Learned Helplessness.* Lexington, MA: D.C. Heath and Co., 1988.

Harding, Sandra. *The Science Question in Feminism.* Ithaca: Cornell University Press, 1986.

Koss, Mary P., Lisa A. Goodman, Angela Browne, Louise F. Fitzgerald, Gwendolyn Puryear Keita, and Nancy Felipe Russo. *No Safe Haven: Male Violence against Women at Home, at Work, and in the Community.* Washington, D.C.: The American Psychological Association, 1994.

LaFave, Wayne R. and Austin W. Scott, Jr. *Criminal Law.* 2nd ed. St. Paul, MN: West Publishing Co., 1986.

Lerman, Lisa. *Prosecution of Spouse Abuse: Innovations in Criminal Justice Response.* Washington, D.C.: Center for Women's Policy Studies, 1981.

Mackinnon, Catherine. *Feminism Unmodified: Discourses on Life and Law.* Cambridge: Harvard University Press, 1987.

Nuttal, Steven D. "An Essay on the Criminal Law Justification Defense," diss., Ohio State University, 1991.

Peterson, Christopher, Steven Maier, and Martin Seligman. *Learned Helplessness: A Theory for the Age of Personal Control.* New York: Oxford University Press, 1993.

Renzetti, Claire. *Violent Betrayal: Partner Abuse in Lesbian Relationships.* Newbury Park, CA: Sage Publications, 1992.

Renzetti, Claire and Raymond Lee, eds. *Researching Sensitive Topics.* Newbury Park, CA: Sage Publications, 1993.

Straus, Murray A., Richard J. Gelles, and Suzanne K. Steinmetz. *Behind Closed Doors: Violence in the American Family.* New York: Anchor Press, 1980.

Walker, Lenore. *The Battered Woman.* New York: Harper & Row, 1979.

———. *The Battered Woman Syndrome.* New York: Springer Publishing, 1984.

——— *Terrifying Love.* New York: Harper & Row, 1989.

Yllo, Kersti and Michelle Bograd, eds. *Feminist Perspectives on Wife Abuse.* Newbury Park, CA: Sage Publications, 1988.

ARTICLES

Astin, Millie C., Kathy J. Lawrence, and David W. Foy. "Posttraumatic Stress Disorder among Battered Women: Risk and Resiliency Factors." *Violence and Victims* 8.1 (1993): 17-28.

Bibliography

Astin, Millie C., Suzann M. Ogland-Hand, Esther M. Coleman, and David W. Foy. "Posttraumatic Stress Disorder and Childhood Abuse in Battered Women: Comparisons with Maritally Distressed Women." *Journal of Consulting and Clinical Psychology* 64.2 (1995): 308-12.

Baumann, Mary A. "Comment: Expert Testimony on the Battered Wife Syndrome: A Question of Admissibility in the Prosecution of the Battered Wife for the Killing of her Husband" (1983). In *Representing . . . . Battered Women Who Kill*, edited by Sara Lee Johann and Frank Osanka. Springfield: Charles C. Thomas, 1989.

Bowker, Lee H. "Battered Wives and the Police: A National Study of Usage and Effectiveness." *Police Studies* 7.2 (Summer 1984).

Browne, Angela. "Violence against Women by Male Partners: Prevalence, Outcomes, and Policy Implications." *American Psychologist* 48.10 (October 1993): 1077-87.

Browne, Angela and Kirk R. Williams. "Race, Resources, and the Reduction of Partner Homicide." *Law and Society Review* 23.1 (1989): 75-94.

Caplan, Gerald. "Getting Away with Murder: How Battered Woman Syndrome is Abused in the Criminal Courts." *Los Angeles Daily Journal*, 28 March 1991, 16.

Cazenave, Noel and Margaret Zahn. "Women, Murder, and Male Domination: Police Reports of Domestic Homicide in Chicago and Philadelphia." Paper presented at the annual meeting of the American Society of Criminology, Atlanta, Georgia, October 1986.

Chittum, Sam, Mark Bauman, and Irene Nyborg-Andersen. "No Way Out." *Ladies Home Journal* 126 (April 1990): 129.

Coffee, Cynthia L. "A Trend Emerges: A State Survey on the Admissibility of Expert Testimony Concerning the Battered Woman Syndrome." *Journal of Family Law* 25 (1986-7): 373-96.

Creach, Donald L. "Note: Partially Determined Self-Defense: The Battered Woman Kills and Tells Why." *Stanford Law Review* 34 (1982): 615-38.

Cross, Meredith. "The Expert as Educator: A Proposed Approach to the Use of Battered Woman Syndrome Expert Testimony." *Vanderbilt Law Review* 35 (1982): 741-68.

Eisenberg, Alan and David Dillon. "Medico-Legal Aspects of Representing the Battered Woman" (1980). In *Representing . . . Battered Women Who Kill*, edited by Sara Lee Johann and Frank Osanka. Springfield: Charles C. Thomas, 1989.

Eisenberg, Alan and Earl Seymour. "Defending the Battered Woman: A Model Voir-Dire." *Trial* (December 1980): 30-3.

John Ellement. "Judge Rules Framingham Eight Member Insane when She Stole." *The Boston Globe*, 20 March 1998, A1.

Faigman, David L. "Notes: The Battered Woman Syndrome and Self-defense: A Legal and Empirical Dissent" (1986). In *Representing . . . Battered Women Who Kill*, edited by Sara Lee Johann and Frank Osanka. Springfield: Charles C. Thomas, 1989.

Follingstad, Diane. "Factors Predicting Verdicts where Battered Women Kill Their Husbands." *Law and Human Behavior* 13.3 (1989): 253-68.

Follingstad, Diane et al. "The Role of Emotional Abuse in Physically Abusive Relationships." *Journal of Family Violence* 5.2 (1990): 113.

Gibbs, Nancy. "'Till Death Do Us Part." *Time*, 18 January 1993, 38-45.

Girdner, Bill. "Justices Balk at 'Battered Woman Syndrome.'" *Los Angeles Daily Journal*, 23 November 1984, 3.

Hart, Barbara J. "State Codes on Domestic Violence: Analysis, Commentary, and Recommendations." *Juvenile and Family Court Journal* 43 (1992).

Houskamp, Beth M. and David W. Foy. "The Assessment of Posttraumatic Stress Disorder in Battered Women." *Journal of Interpersonal Violence* 6.3 (1991): 367-75.

Kemp, Anita, Edna I. Rawlings, and Bonnie L. Green. "Post-Traumatic Stress Disorder in Battered Women: A Shelter Sample." *Journal of Traumatic Stress* 4.1 (1991): 137-48.

Kobil, Daniel T. "The Quality of Mercy Strained: Wresting the Pardoning Power from the King." *Texas Law Review* 69.3 (February 1991): 569-641.

———. "Do the Paperwork or Die: Clemency, Ohio Style?" *Ohio State Law Journal* 52.3 (June 1991): 655-704.

Latour, Francie. "Happy Endings Elude the Framingham Eight." *The Boston Sunday Globe*, 15 February 1998, A1.

Lewin, Tamar. "More States Study Clemency for Women Who Killed Abusers." *The New York Times*, 21 February 1991, A19.

Locy, Toni. "Weld Urged to Free Eight Women: Commutations Sought for Inmates Who Killed Alleged Abusers." *The Boston Globe*, 15 February 1992, 15.

———. "Weld Backs Commutation for Four Inmates: One Says Man She Killed Was Her Batterer." *The Boston Globe*, 21 January 1993, 29.

Johnson, Carla Ann Hage. "Entitled to Clemency: Mercy in the Criminal Law." *Law and Philosophy* 10 (1991): 109-18.

Johnson, John M. and Kathleen J. Ferraro. "The Victimized Self: The Case of Battered Women." In *The Existential Self in Society*, edited by Joséph A. Kotawba and Andrea Fontana. Chicago: The University of Chicago Press, 1984.

Mahoney, Martha R. "Legal Images of Battered Women: Redefining the Issue of Separation." *Michigan Law Review* 90.1 (October, 1991): 1-94.

Mann, Coramae R. "Getting Even? Women Who Kill in Domestic Encounters" (1988). In *Representing . . . Battered Women Who Kill*, edited by Sara Lee Johann and Frank Osanka. Springfield: Charles C. Thomas, 1989.

National Clearinghouse for the Defense of Battered Women. "Battered Women Who Have Received Clemency: 1978-1996." Draft report, Philadelphia, PA: January 1998.

National Coalition Against Domestic Violence. "National Estimates and Facts about Domestic Abuse." *NCADV Voice* (Winter 1989): 12.

O'Keefe, Maura. "Posttraumatic Stress Disorder among Battered Women: A Comparison of Battered Women Who Killed Their Abusers and Those Incarcerated for Other Offenses." *Journal of Traumatic Stress* 11.1 (1998): 71-85.

Reinharz, Shulamit. "The Social Psychology of a Miscarriage: An Application of Symbolic Interaction Theory and Method." In *Women and Symbolic Interaction*, edited by Mary Jo Deegan and Michael Hill. Boston: Allen & Unwin, Inc., 1987.

Renzetti, Claire. "Building a Second Closet: Third Party Responses to Victims of Lesbian Partner Abuse." In *Understanding Partner Violence: Prevalence, Causes, Consequences, & Solutions*, edited by Sandra M. Stith and Murray A. Straus. Minneapolis: National Council on Family Relations, 1995.

Romero, Mary "A Comparison between Strategies Used on Prisoners of War and Abused Wives." *Sex Roles* 13 (1985): 537-47.

Schneider, Elizabeth M. "Equal Rights to Trial for Women: Sex Bias in the Law of Self-Defense." *Harvard Civil Rights-Civil Liberties Law Review* 50 (Winter 1980): 623-47.

——. "Describing and Changing: Women's Self-Defense Work and the Problem of Expert Testimony on Battering" (1986). In *Representing . . . Battered Women Who Kill*, edited by Sara Lee Johann and Frank Osanka. Springfield: Charles C. Thomas, 1989.

——. "Particularity and Generality." *New York University Law Review* 67 (June 1992): 520-68.

Snitow, Ann. "A Gender Diary." In *Conflicts in Feminism*, edited by Marianne Hirsch and Evelyn Keller. New York: Routledge, 1990.

Straus, Murray A. and Richard J. Gelles. "Societal Change in Family Violence from 1975 to 1985 as Revealed by Two National Surveys. In *Understanding Partner Violence: Prevalence, Causes, Consequences, & Solutions*, edited by Sandra M. Stith and Murray A. Straus. Minneapolis: National Council on Family Relations, 1995.

Thyfault, Roberta K. "Self-Defense: Battered Woman Syndrome on Trial" (1984). In *Representing . . . Battered Women Who Kill*, edited by Sara Lee Johann and Frank Osanka. Springfield: Charles C. Thomas, 1989.

Walker, Lenore E. "Post-Traumatic Stress Disorder in Women: Diagnosis and Treatment of Battered Woman Syndrome." *Psychotherapy* 28.1 (Spring 1991): 21-9.

Walus-Wigle, Jacqueline and J. Reid Meloy. "Battered Woman Syndrome as a Criminal Defense." *Journal of Psychology and Law* 16 (Fall 1988): 389-404.

Young, Iris M. "The Ideal of Community and the Politics of Difference." In *Feminism/Postmodernism*, edited by Linda Nicholson. New York: Routledge, 1990.

GOVERNMENT PUBLICATIONS

Dutton, Mary Ann. "Impact of Evidence Concerning Battering and Its Effects in Criminal Trials Involving Battered Women." In *The Validity and Use of Evidence Concerning Battering and Its Effects in Criminal Trials*. Report Responding to Section 40507 of the Violence Against Women Act. Washington, D.C.: U.S. Department of Justice and U.S. Department of Health and Human Services, May 1996, NCJ 160972.

Fagan, Jeffrey. *The Criminalization of Domestic Violence: Promises and Limits*. National Institute of Justice Research Report. Washington, D.C., January 1996.

Parrish, Janet. "Trend Analysis: Expert Testimony on Battering and Its Effects in Criminal Cases." In *The Validity and Use of Evidence Concerning Battering and Its Effects in Criminal Trials*. Report Responding to Section 40507 of the Violence Against Women Act. Washington, D.C.: U.S. Department of Justice and U.S. Department of Health and Human Services, May 1996, NCJ 160972.

U.S. Commission on Civil Rights. *Under the Rule of Thumb: Battered Women and the Administration of Justice*. Washington, D.C., January 1982.

U.S. Department of Health and Human Services. *Preventing Violence Against Women*. Fact sheet. Washington, D.C., May 1998.

U.S. Department of Justice. *Final Report of the Attorney General's Task Force on Domestic Violence*. Washington, D.C., 1984.

U.S. Department of Justice. Bureau of Justice Statistics. *Report to the Nation*. 2nd ed. Washington, D.C., March 1988.

———. *Violence Between Intimates: Domestic Violence*. Washington, D.C., November 1994, NCJ 149259.

———. *Spouse Murder Defendants in Large Urban Counties*. Washington, D.C., September 1995, NCJ 156831.

———. *Violence by Intimates: Analysis of Data on Crimes by Current or Former Spouses, Boyfriends, and Girlfriends.* Washington, D.C., March 1998, NCJ 167237.

U. S. Department of Justice. Federal Bureau of Investigation. *Uniform Crime Reports for 1983.* Washington, D.C., 1984.

U.S. Senate Judiciary Committee. *Women and Violence: Hearings before the U.S. Senate Judiciary Committee.* Senate Hearing 101-939, pt. 2, 29 August 1990 and 11 December 1990.

LEGAL DOCUMENTS

Booker, Shannon. "Personal Statement to the Governor: Clemency Petition." Boston, MA: 14 February 1992.

Domestic Violence Council. "Brief in Support of Petitions for Commutation. (In the Matter of Commutation Petitions of Patricia Allen, Shannon Booker, Lisa Grimshaw, Patricia Hennessy, Elaine Hyde, Eugenia Moore, Deborah Reid, and Meekah Scott)." Boston, MA: 19 February 1992.

Grimshaw, Lisa. "Personal Statement to the Governor: Clemency Petition." Boston, MA: 14 February 1992.

Hennessy, Patricia. "Personal Statement to the Governor: Clemency Petition." Boston, MA: 14 February 1992.

Hyde, Elaine. "Personal Statement to the Governor: Clemency Petition." Boston, MA: 14 February 1992.

Massachusetts Executive Department. "Commutation Guidelines and Petition." Boston, MA: September 1991.

The Violence Against Women Act of 1994. Title IV of the Violent Crime Control and Law Enforcement Act. Public Law 103-322.

CASES

Dyas v. United States, 376 A.2d 827 (D.C. 1977).
Fennell v. Goolsby, 630 F. Supp. 451 (E. D. Pa. 1985).
Fulgham v. State, 46 Ala. 143 (1871)
Ibn-Tamas v. United States, 407 A. 2d 626 (D.C. 1979).
People v. Garcia, Cr. No. 4259 (Superior Court, Monterey County, CA, 1977).
People v. Torres, 488 N.Y.S. 2d 358, 128 Misc. 2d 129 (Sup. 1985).
State v. Hodges, 716 P. 2d 566, 239 Kan. 63 (Kan. 1986).
State v. Hundley, 693 P. 2d 475, 236 Kan. 461 (Kan. 1985).

State v. Kelly, 478 A. 2d 364, 97 N.J. 178 (N.J. 1984).
State v. Wanrow, 549 P. 2d 548, 88 Wash. 2d 221 (Wash. 1977).

OTHER SOURCES

Booker, Shannon. Interview by author. Tape recording. Framingham, MA, 26 June 1993.
Browne, Angela. Interview by author. Boston, MA, 12 October 1993.
Cordy, Bob. Interview by author. Boston, MA, 21 June 1993.
Grimshaw, Lisa. Interview by author. Tape recording. Lancaster, MA, 11 April 1993 and 17 June 1993.
Hennessy, Patricia. Interview by author. Tape recording. Framingham, MA, 26 June 1993.
Hyde, Elaine. Interview by author. Tape recording. Lancaster, MA, 11 April 1993 and 18 June 1993.
Schneider, Elizabeth. Telephone conversation with author, 6 October 1993.

ABOUT THE AUTHOR

Amy Busch is a doctoral student in clinical psychology at the University of California, Berkeley.